Lessons from the Trenches

Lessons from the Trenches

Perspectives of a survivor CIO

By Al Venslovaitis

CIO Advisors

Toronto

2015

Some names and identifying details have been changed to protect the privacy of individuals.

First Printing: 2015

ISBN

Print: 978-0-9948442-0-0

ePub: 978-0-9948442-1-7

Mobi: 978-0-9948442-2-4

Cover Illustration reprinted by permission of RareHistoricalPhotos.com

Editing by John C.P. King

CIO Advisors
4 – 2130 Dickson Road
Mississauga, Ontario L5B1Y6 Canada

To all information technology professionals. May we achieve and receive the recognition that we earn.

ABOUT THE AUTHOR

For 20 years, Al Venslovaitis was a successful CIO with five Canadian multinational corporations – Sherritt Gordon Mines, Canada Wire and Cable, the interior systems group of Magna International, de Havilland Division of Bombardier Aerospace Group and The Globe and Mail. In these roles he worked with the Executive Team to develop an IT strategy and to carry it out, usually within challenging financial constraints.

From 1999 until 2011, Al was an IT management consultant providing clients advice on how to make successful investments in Information Technology. He advised clients on IT strategy, and helped them to implement key initiatives often in the role of their interim or part-time CIO.

Most recently, from 2011 through 2014, Al was employed at the Greater Toronto Airports Authority (GTAA) as the Director in charge of IT Strategic Alignment and IT Solution Delivery, completing his tenure finally as Acting CIO.

INTENDED AUDIENCE

This book is written primarily for those who aspire to become a CIO sometime in the future and for those in the executive management or of the direction of the enterprise who aspire to fill the role with someone likely to succeed. In all cases, I believe this book will provide such aspirants with the means to determine the presence or absence of important knowledge and attitudes.

It is intended for, and is likely also to be of assistance to those who are occupying the position for the first time. People in that situation will be expected to put their own stamp on the IT function in relatively short order. The usual expectation is within 60 to 100 days. This book will provide them with ideas as to the priority areas to apply improvements for relatively quick and beneficial effect.

Finally, it may even be of assistance to relatively experienced CIOs who may already be in their second or subsequent mandate.

Comments and feedback are welcome from anyone who reads this book. Kindly address it to the author at: a@cioadvisors.ca.

INTRODUCTION

Why write this book? Or more to the point from your perspective, why read it?

If you are, or aspire to be a Chief Information Officer (CIO), or you are a senior executive contemplating hiring a new CIO, please bear with me for a few pages and I'll try to persuade you. The rest of you are excused.

The average period of service for a CIO has been, and continues to be, relatively short. Until the recent habit of quickly replacing Chief Executive Officers after a relatively few years in office became all the rage, it was the CIO, or Chief Information Officer role that held the track record for the shortest-tenured executive position in any substantial organization. And it's still pretty close. Why is that? What drives the CIO mortality rate, and why is the tenure of the senior IT executive so short? This small book is full of practical reasons explaining why that is so, and with practical tips on how a new CIO can extend her/his tenure to the point where it is a personal decision to depart for greener pastures. So please, read on.

Quite a few years ago, CIO = "Career Is Over" was the not so funny alias assigned to the acronym and the rather black humour still, woefully, enjoys wide currency to this day.

I personally "enjoyed" an introduction to this redefined title in 1996 after joining The Globe and Mail – Canada's National Newspaper – as the Vice-President, Information Technology. Almost immediately after I took up my new duties, I and my C-level colleagues, including the Publisher and CEO attended a technology conference put on by a sister company – Thomson Technologies. My colleagues initially found much of the conference rather dull, so they started to amuse themselves by passing notes around the darkened auditorium. I received one entitled "for the Career Is Over, provide survival estimate." In the spirit of fair play, I was also required to enter a guess. The results were tabulated and averaged at the coffee break. Now, well after my departure from The Globe, I am pleased to report that I beat the average prediction by quite a margin. But then ... the prediction average was extraordinarily short.

So it's no great surprise that quite a body of literature entitled "CIO Survival Guide," or some close variant has developed over the past five to 10 years. (Had such a guide been available in the late 1990s I would have certainly made use of it.) The books provide a range of advice, from specific technologies to adopt, to quite thoughtful descriptions of the role of the Chief Information Officer and how s/he can best discharge it. While doubtless useful and interesting, I find it strange that none of these many books (to my knowledge) has actually been written by someone who did the job.

For this reason, I thought it would be useful (and enjoyable) to put my hand to the task. For more than 20 years I filled the role of the CIO for a number of Canadian multinational companies, most of which had extensive operations in the United States and some of which also operated in the United Kingdom and elsewhere in the world. Since those days I have been an IT management consultant, filling in interim and part-time CIO positions, advising and assisting CIOs and in other ways helping my clients make successful investments in information technology. Although more than a little battered and scarred, after about 30 years in the business I would characterize myself as a CIO survivor. More or less.

I bring the sympathies, perspective and experience of a CIO to this book, but it is not intended to merely be a survival guide for the CIO (although that is a likely by-product). It will describe what a properly operating information technology function within a medium to large corporation should look like. It also makes an effort to describe what the ecosystem for a successful IT function should look like. The intent therefore is for the incumbent CIO and her/his colleagues to work co-operatively at shaping both to achieve success.

Introduction

The great underlying assumption of this book is that the achievement of results – of adding significant business value – is the prime IT directive. Many CIOs have survived for very long periods on political skills alone. In no way do I disparage these specific "soft skills" of managing up to the CEO and the Board of Directors. They are without a doubt important to the longevity of any executive, and anyone at senior levels in any organization who is worth her/his salt must develop them to a considerable extent. However, this book does not provide any guidance in this regard. The focus is results. "Il nous faut des résultats, encore des résultats, et toujours des résultats" to paraphrase Frederick the Great and/or Napoleon – both of whom were rather good survivors.

So why is something so blindingly obvious being emphasized? Well, for three reasons.

First, because I don't believe that there exists a generally accepted, simple, practical and comprehensive model for the management of the IT function. There are large elements of it – chiefly provided by the Project Management Institute (PMI) and by the Information Technology Infrastructure Library (ITIL). There is the rather overly comprehensive model provided by the ISO 38500 standard for IT Governance. But there is no easily comprehended and pragmatically useful model that bears all three of the attributes in the first sentence. This is what is offered in the body of this book.

Second, because I am personally quite discouraged by how poorly IT is regarded "out there," and how oftentimes the poor opinion is well-earned. I am proud of my profession; I believe that it can and does do very well in many places and much of the time. Perhaps I am delusional. But I fervently hope that through a sharing of my experiences as a CIO "in the trenches," of what I found works and what doesn't, I may help the IT profession improve its delivery performance and thereby its reputation.

Third, because IT itself is so new. There has been very little time (relatively to Finance, Engineering, Operations and other organizational functions) for a comprehensive model to be evolved, generally accepted, and broadly followed. This is intended as a modest but well-intentioned contribution toward the IT function's maturation.

It seems strange in these days to find that Information Technology as a specific term used in the modern sense dates back to a Harvard Business Review article published in 1958. In those days "information technology" was an interesting curiosity. Now, in the second decade of the 21st century, it is by far the most important activity engaged in globally, as measured by the value of professional services, hardware and software sold annually. It surpassed the mighty automotive industry in this regard more than a decade ago and the gap continues to widen.

For a long time now, it has been a cliché that IT permeates all aspects of our lives. It is recognized as a strategic tool for economic well-being, for reducing costs, reducing cycle times, improving quality, for providing services that could not otherwise be delivered, for bringing better new products to market faster, and indeed for providing competitive advantage of all kinds. In countless ways, the invention and continuing development of IT has been a great boon to the modern enterprise.

Yet paradoxically at the same time, everywhere there is evidence that IT is managed poorly. While there are shining examples of IT success stories put forward by CIO Magazine among many other sources, these seem to be the exception that proves the rule. For every success story there are multiple horror stories.

The Standish Group – an international IT research firm – regularly and depressingly reports that only about one-third of all large IT projects are completed on time, on budget and delivering all the promised capabilities. That means two-thirds of them fail by one or more of these three basic criteria. Of late, there has been some organized criticism of the Standish Group's report, accusing it of being biased because it has an axe to grind, or that it is interpreting the results far too harshly. I take no sides in this dispute, but I simply observe that in general – again with exceptions – most users of IT services have no respect for the organizations delivering them, and in some cases absolutely and very openly despise them. One reason has to be this perception, and perhaps it's an actual fact, that IT organizations are very poor at delivering successful results.

From the perspective and experience of this former CIO, it isn't all that difficult to establish and maintain a high-performing IT function. Most of what is written here to make that happen is no mystery to any seasoned CIO, and in many cases there may be better ideas and experiences available, than those I set out (if anyone thinks so, please do me the favour of getting in touch and sharing). Even in the case of a seasoned CIO, I believe that I am providing somewhere in this document at least one idea or one set of experiences that if adopted or adapted will improve his/her performance. As late as my fifth incarnation as a CIO at The Globe and Mail, one single idea (which alas, I only learned after I left The Globe), if it had been provided to me in a publication such as this, would have made a huge positive difference both to my longevity and to the enterprise that I served.

Much has been thought and written about the business value of computing, the total cost of ownership of investments in IT, determining the necessary and sufficient conditions for an enterprise to employ an executive-level manager responsible for the IT establishment (CIO) and about objective measures of the success of investments in IT. Most of this large and useful output has come from academics, from bystanders and from specialists. Very little if anything has been written from the point of view of the practitioner – that is from the point of view of the Chief Information Officer who has been in the trenches, and has had the opportunity to learn lessons from life's two greatest teachers – success and failure.

This book was written to provide such a perspective so that corporate executive management, CIOs and those aspiring to be CIOs, might derive some benefit from those experiences.

Al Venslovaitis

Toronto

July 2015

TABLE OF CONTENTS

Table of contents

TABLE OF FIGURES

CHAPTER 1 BASIC TRUTHS

This section on "basic truths" sets out the fundamental ideas and attitudes that I consider to be essential to the success of an aspiring CIO. The reader is encouraged to consider them as essential elements to success. Ignore them at your peril.

Perspective

It was my very great and good fortune some years ago to be employed as the CIO of The Globe and Mail, Canada's National Newspaper. The management and staff of this organization made up by far the most intellectual, the liveliest and the wittiest group of people I was ever privileged to work with. Hard work was often leavened by hard play.

One day there was a break in a very intense meeting that involved a broad group of management somewhat weighted numerically toward the editorial function. Somehow a debate started regarding "What is news?" It went on for some time, beginning with serious intent, but gradually becoming more hilarious and rather raucous.

Finally – because it was time to get back to business – Roger Parkinson, the Publisher and CEO, stepped in and said, "I'll settle this! I'll tell you what 'news' is." He looked around the room as he waited for silence. Then he said, "It's whatever I see around me that looks like news. In short, it's what I say it is!" Somehow he retained control of the meeting and we returned to the original agenda.

What is good enough for Roger is certainly good enough for me. So this is very much a personal view of how IT should view itself, and how it should be managed. It is based on much that is written by scholars of the subject and by conventional wisdom in the field, but mostly it's presented from my very own perspective and experiences.

I make no claims to the one true way to organize and run an effective IT function. There are bound to be other effective ways, more or less similar to the model that I will be sharing with you.

Chapter 1 Basic truths

The key is that this is my way. It is the way I learned how to do the job, through both positive lessons and negative ones – my own personal experience. Others likely had somewhat different experiences, and I hope that this book prompts them to come forward to speak about their own experiences and what worked for them. In the meantime, these are my own perspectives and where possible I try to illustrate points I'm making with anecdotes.

As a start, I have set out the following basic issues and themes as I have observed them firsthand and internalized their lessons over several decades first as a CIO and then as an IT management consultant.

These really are – in my view – the basic truths. If a CIO and her/his organization have not already mastered the following points, then they are unlikely to be unsuccessful until they make a conscious effort to do so.

The role of IT

Some people believe in a mission statement for IT, and have done some interesting work in articulating such a thing. Personally, I think a corporation, or any other independent enterprise can benefit greatly from clear statements of a mission, vision and values but a constituent functional organization within the enterprise simply needs a clear statement of its role within the greater enterprise.

Whether mission or role, it's the utility of the thing, not its label which is important. The following, or variants, emerged quite some time ago, and I believe it continues to provide a useful description of what IT should be doing for your enterprise. IT's role is:

To deliver the right information
to the right person
in the right place
at the right time
in the right form
for the right cost.

Reliable "delivery" is the reason why organizations have an expensive IT department. It's what IT does. Everything else is just details.

Chapter 1 Basic truths

Intrinsic value of information technology

To put it briefly and bluntly – there is none. There is no intrinsic value to information technology. All of its value (or lack thereof) derives completely from the purpose the enterprise originally envisioned for a particular IT investment, how successfully it is used by the organization that invests in it, and how successfully the investment helps to achieve whatever outcome the enterprise had in mind.

The business derives value from information technology by using the capabilities provided to do things in a "faster, better, cheaper" manner. Thereby the business achieves competitive advantage through incremental market share, or revenue or through cost savings that are made possible – "enabled" – by the IT investment, or allowing entry into new markets (e.g. Internet sales), or some other outcome that requires an investment in some form of IT to make it possible.

Understanding and internalizing that a successful investment in information technology is a two-stage process and that both stages require a close collaboration between the business users and IT Delivery team is the key to the success of any investment in information technology.

In other words, the business must visualize and articulate what it needs to achieve. IT provides suggestions as to ways and means this could be done using the technology. If one of the suggestions has merit, it is adopted and the investment is made to provide the means. The business value is in the achievement of the business result. There is no value to the IT investment until and unless the business is able to deliver on its original vision by putting the new IT asset to work.

Understanding and internalizing this fundamental fact is the key to success for any CIO and her/his team. It provides a useful framework from which to understand what decisions are owned by the IT functions and which cannot be; who calls which shots while

IT assets are created; and who calls which shots while they are operated and maintained during the period that they are in service.

Chapter 1 Basic truths

The IT department is almost universally hated. Why?

There is no hiding from this fact.

While I was a working CIO, I had an inkling of this, but I deluded myself that this universal frustration and lack of trust and respect was a local phenomenon. I thought it was out of the norm – something that was temporarily not right with the world until I fixed it for the anomalous enterprise that just happened to be employing me at the time. Not so.

I began to fully understand the breadth and depth of this almost universal contempt for the internal IT organization during my years as a management consultant. While earning my spurs at the Osborne Group as a specialist in IT-specific management matters, I had to learn how to "hustle up" new business. As a step in that education, I accepted what turned out to be brilliant advice from the founder and owner – Don "Osborne" Wood. He told me to simply assume that this fear and loathing of one's own internal IT function was universal, and offer prospective client contacts an "IT diagnostic" to identify and fix the IT issues that ailed the client's business. It turned out to be one of my best sources of new clients, and indeed a fairly robust consulting practice on its own.

Along the way it became quite clear to me why there was such a dysfunctional relationship between IT and the rest of the enterprise it purported to serve. Essentially it was because the management of most IT functions has failed to grasp and master the basics outlined in this little book.

Read on.

Business process

The disciplined management of business process and the successful investment in information technology go hand in hand. For a much more eloquent explanation of this than I could possibly manage, I refer the reader to the book "Faster, Better, Cheaper" by Michael Hammer and Lisa W. Hershman (Crown Publishing, 2010).

In most instances the business case for investment in new IT is based on the enablement of improved business processes. Yet the general lack of understanding of the meaning and importance of business process improvement inside the IT function is still depressingly widespread. (Even more depressing is how poorly understood or appreciated it is in business management generally, outside of a very few industries.)

Before I am pilloried or otherwise excoriated by legions of earnest and outraged IT business systems analysts, let me make myself clear. I am not saying that IT (especially its business analysts) are unfamiliar with business processes, how they are described and how they are modelled. My point is that the language and use of business process by IT is largely descriptive – in business requirements documents primarily. Furthermore, business process is rarely subjected by IT staff to analysis of process capabilities, and even less often does IT put forward prescriptive measures intended to improve the outcomes of the business process under study. In fact, often IT groups make it a point of standard operating practice not to "infringe" upon business responsibilities – which in their thinking includes sole responsibility for their (the business's) own processes. In my view, that's a mistake. It confuses accountability for business process, with the capability within IT to offer quantified insight and advice on how the business process "machine" can be improved for the client.

To be clear: accountability for the effective functioning of business process of course rests with the business. On the other hand, it is a useful element of engagement for IT to work itself into a position where it has the competence to suggest ideas for the improvement of business process outcomes.

Of course, where good ideas come from within the overall organization is irrelevant, as long as they're competently evaluated and acted upon in a timely fashion. Indeed it makes sense for a lot of reasons – local knowledge and easiest buy-in being two obvious ones – for most business process improvement ideas to come from the business area involved. (That doesn't mean IT shouldn't be trying to plant seeds!)

The issue isn't so much who in the organization champions good business process improvement ideas, or where the Six Sigma or Lean black belts reside. It is in the readiness and professionalism of IT to recognize, evaluate and finally to embrace such ideas as they bubble up.

Too often, IT has to be persuaded and then educated to IT investment opportunities, and is a "Johnny come lately" to the substantive discussions of ways and means to realize the desired results. This has the effect of delaying investment decisions and creating the appearance of IT as an obstructive group, even if often it genuinely is not intending to be so.

How much better for everyone involved, if the CIO and her/his direct reports were to get out in front of such discussions and indeed if they made a special effort to facilitate or even sponsor a relentless and ongoing search for "faster, better, cheaper" ways of doing business.

This requires an investment of time to learn about the organization's businesses and about its current practices in carrying out those businesses. It also requires an investment of time to learn "enough" about Six Sigma, Lean methodologies, Hammer & Co. methodologies, and any other business process improvement approaches that may be appropriate for the organization, or already in vogue within it. It may require some considerable investment of time "evangelizing" to the rest of the organization about the value and benefits of a formal and disciplined approach to business process. Finally, it definitely requires an investment of time and imagination for ways and means "to be seen" as facilitating business process improvement.

There is no formula, or "one size fits all" approach to get oneself into such a position that I'm aware of. There are some illustrative examples of steps taken toward this goal later in this volume, but each senior IT management team must figure out how to create both this reality and its perception within its own organizational culture. It's not rocket science to do so. Nurture whatever parts of the greater organization house black belts of process improvement methodologies. Create or support one or more forums for its discussion. Be good listeners. Celebrate business process successes (especially those where IT made the difference – after all, we need to take care of our <u>own</u> business). Hold workshops or symposiums on a regular basis. Talk it up, and be seen to talk it up, developing allies and champions along the way. It's essentially a form of networking.

However they set about doing it, the IT leadership team – the CIO and her/his direct reports – should make it their business to establish themselves as the "go to" people for brainstorming, nurturing and developing good ideas for business process improvement.

Is it plausible that the CIO achieving such an outcome will be well-regarded? Will s/he and his/her leadership team wield influence and command respect? Will all of this be deserved? Absolutely yes to all three.

On an even more selfish, parochial note, many (but absolutely not all) of those ideas will require capital investment in new IT, and as such will be an ongoing source of "new business" for IT. What's more, solidly based on the applied arts of business process improvement, a portfolio of these projects will greatly outperform the much-lamented "Standish average" (See the Introduction) and bring even more lustre to the IT function.

Customer service and client relations

We spoke a little earlier about the undesirability of IT appearing to be an obstacle to progress. Dilbert – the popular comic strip – on occasion features a character named "Mordac the preventer of information services." While clearly an amusing exaggeration, this character taps into a deeply held perception of IT practitioners' attitudes to client relations and customer service.

It is sad but true that there is a widespread antipathy toward IT departments. And there is an equally widespread distrust of their motives and methods. Mordac – and the rest of his dastardly colleagues in IT – appear to be able to spend obscene amounts of money without delivering any tangible benefits to the organization. Moreover they seem able to avoid being held to account with impunity. What really disheartens internal clients is that there seem never to be any consequences to bad attitudes and poor service.

It's downright depressing to observe that many otherwise intelligent IT executives fail to make the obvious connection. The more Mordac-like performers there are in their department, and the longer they seem to abide without being brought to account, the more ineffectual, foolish and incompetent the CIO and IT management in general is perceived to be. Under those circumstances, would that perception be unjust?

To be fair most people may need some extra help to make the penny drop. (Perhaps they should read a good book on IT management?) In my case, I was lucky enough to get some helpful coaching on a very useful technique for holding IT accountable – very visibly – from a superior and from a peer.

On my first day as CIO for de Havilland Division of Boeing Commercial Aircraft Group, after the obligatory initial briefing from my new boss (let's call him Kingsley), he informed me that we were going to meet my outgoing predecessor in the plant.

Chapter 1 Basic truths

Kingsley gave me a guided tour of the operation from the Administration building on the south side of the campus, to the Final Assembly Bay at least a kilometre away on the north side, passing through various detail fabrication and sub-assembly shops on the way. I was then introduced to my predecessor (let's call him Chuck), who was going to be transferred back to Seattle after a bit of an overlap with me. Kingsley went off on his own business, while Chuck gave me a tour in reverse through parts of the plant I had not seen until we finally ended up in his (now my) office on the south side of the campus again.

Interestingly, by the time we got to my office it was end of day – sometime after 6 p.m., and I had reported promptly at 8 a.m. All the IT staff had already left, and it was too late for introductions to my new direct reports, which would now have to wait for the next day. I remarked that it was a very long walk across a very large manufacturing operation.

Chuck agreed and asked whether I had noticed any other reason for the length of time taken. I noted that both he and Kingsley stopped frequently to chat with various people along the way and that seemed to take up a considerable amount of time. Chuck commended me for noticing, and then pointed out that, while it all looked very social and informal, there was a serious purpose to the banter.

Chuck had been transferred to de Havilland in Toronto from the Boeing Commercial Aircraft head office in Seattle for a short-term fill-in assignment while a local CIO (who turned out to be me) was recruited to replace Kingsley, who had been promoted to a broader role that included IT. Chuck's assignment was estimated to be for about six months. He knew that the IT department at de Havilland had many problems and was poorly regarded. He wanted to take some positive action, but he knew he didn't have the time or the mandate to do a thorough analysis, or to make a lot of sweeping changes. What to do?

In the end, he chose to focus exclusively on building bridges with the clients of IT – which was virtually everyone, as it is in most organizations. A daily walk in the plant, making himself accessible and approachable to anyone who chose to speak to him – to complain or to float ideas – turned out to be the most effective tool. By acting on all these interactions, either solving problems or managing expectations, he felt he had built useful bridges to many clients, and strongly recommended that I continue the process.

I took the advice to heart and followed it to my everlasting benefit. I recommend it to any other IT executive: make building and maintaining friendly relations with all your clients your first priority.

While we're on the topic of client relations, it's appropriate to understand that good quality work – and good service – are entirely determined by your clients' perception. Your client is the sole arbiter of what constitutes good quality. Your opinion of how well you are performing, or your staff's, or your vendors' if you have substantially outsourced IT services, are entirely incidental. I'll state it as a truism here, something I learned from my days as a CIO in the automotive business. If you don't accept it, or understand it, read up on the subject of quality. Convince yourself and embrace it. It is both a clarifying and a liberating idea. If you aren't convinced, then just trust me on this one.

Another simple but helpful idea to embrace is: "What you permit, you promote." This harkens to my more recent days as a member of the IT leadership team at the Greater Toronto Airports Authority. My boss the CIO brought it to my attention, without taking any particular credit for its origin. When I first heard the phrase, I felt I understood the value of the concept behind it. Apart from illustrating that old guys can still learn new ideas and new perspectives, the phrase harkens back to the "Mordac" conversation earlier in this section. If you as the CIO, or your IT leadership team, allow bad behaviour and bad performance to persist, then it is assumed that you support it and promote it. So you all wear it.

There is of course, a lot more to customer service and client relations. A CIO must be seen to foster transparency and accountability. Performance measures must be in place to support this. And so on, as is expounded upon later in this book. Only if you walk the walk are you fully entitled to talk the talk.

Just think anti-Mordac.

Management education, training, experience

It's quite common for new managers in certain staff groups (e.g. finance, design engineering, facilities management, and of course information technology) to have had very little management education, training or experience. Their focus at the start of their careers is on mastering the technical subject matter of their professions, and properly so. Once they have achieved a level of stature in their profession, and are given the opportunity to manage teams of their professional peers, then lack of management savvy becomes an issue and must be remedied.

While this is doubtless a similar situation for all back office and support functions, for some reason it seems to be most acute in information technology. Information technology organizations seem to have less appreciation for or understanding of management principles and the management arts and sciences. It isn't unusual to encounter substantial IT establishments where all of the senior management tend to be very weak in leadership, in personnel management, in the delegation of responsibility, in customer service practices, in providing actionable feedback to under- or over-performing staff, or any of the other basic management skills.

Inexperienced management at the top levels of IT is a serious obstacle to progress. Not only is it unable to provide competent leadership for the vital IT roles of alignment and delivery (about which more later), it is also incapable of effectively delegating the elements of it to the staff who might be able to deliver. It also removes any realistic opportunity for useful role models. It creates infertile ground for internal or external coaching and mentoring. Thus there is no realistic prospect of improving management capability among middle and junior management, where it is critically needed.

An IT function in the hands of people untrained in or inexperienced in management, is going to be mismanaged. It will almost inevitably be inefficient and ineffective. It will thereby reinforce the widespread negative perception of IT. And just incidentally it will waste opportunities for competitive advantage or will cause real damage to the competitiveness of the enterprise affected, or both.

Moreover, weak management at the top provides a template suitable for replication everywhere else in the IT organization. To prevent a vast wasteland of deadwood in the management of your IT division, a necessary requirement is that the CIO be an excellent manager who is also a good fit for your corporate culture.

The larger the corporation and the more dependent it is on an effective IT function for success – maintaining cost-effectiveness and developing competitive advantage – then the riskier it is to have a rookie (i.e. a person inexperienced in the management of a functional group of a similar size) in the CIO's role. Too many large organizations throw some poor soul into the water and hope s/he doesn't drown. There are more reliable and less destructive ways to develop the talent pool – sometimes one of the lame excuses for offering up a sacrificial lamb in such a manner – than by putting a rookie in charge.

The CIO must be a seasoned veteran with a track record of success – not only at leading a substantial IT function for a large organization, but especially at developing an effective management team.

It is not difficult to determine whether the incumbent is such a person. And if a determination is made that s/he is not, then a replacement should be sought humanely – but immediately. Or an intelligent and structured process – with frequent off ramps – should be immediately put in place to coach, mentor and develop this person's capabilities to become an effective IT leader and executive. Better yet, knowing in advance of the lack of experience and management skills, why make the appointment in the first place without putting such support and development mechanisms in place?

Surely these are self-evident facts. Surely the absence of specific experience and of specific training are also easily and factually knowable. So then why do large organizations set up these conditions for failure by putting rookies in the CIO role and then simply watching them fail?

It is instructive to note that venture capitalists and angel investors never invest in an entrepreneurial new venture unless it is headed by a management team that has successfully launched a start-up before. In my efforts to raise funding for software start-ups in years past, I learned that this is the first criterion they look at. If it's not met, they invariably pass, and another good idea doesn't see the light of day. Their rationale is that there is no lack of good ideas, but there is a depressingly consistent rate of failure to convert these ideas into a money-making enterprise if they are not brought to market by people who know what they're doing.

Why should IT – the greatest engine your organization has for transformational change – be looked at any differently?

Performance measurement and accountability

The "walkabout" described in an earlier section is one of many tactics that IT executives can use to set a tone. It puts out a welcome mat to the client base, and lets them know that whatever else goes on in IT that they will get an open and friendly hearing from the leadership. Unless the shop is so small that everything can be managed as an exception, the IT leadership must also be working continuously on the discipline and professionalism of the rest of IT in order to keep these exceptions to a minimum.

Management educator and author Peter Drucker once said, "What gets measured, gets managed." I think the paraphrase, "What is not measured is not managed," explains the need more pointedly to the management-averse IT function.

In IT as in many other business areas, there is no lack of things to measure. The challenge – also not unique to IT management – is to determine the few significant and relevant elements to manage well and therefore to measure.

In my "IT diagnostic" practice, I have probed for the presence or absence of measurement in the IT function. If there was formal performance measurement (not that common a thing), then I probed for the nature of the measurement. If there was a strong correlation between what was measured and its relevance to holding IT accountable to its customers, then I knew that my advice would probably be unnecessary. Whatever opportunities for improvement I would have found were almost certainly already known (or soon would be, without my intervention) to IT management, and to their colleagues in the rest of the organization.

Otherwise, I start a list of "observations" (a.k.a. "problems" requiring solution) and probe in other directions to start populating a very pointed list of things to fix. In my experience the list will include a lot of fundamental problems. No matter how or how much IT measures itself, if it is not subject to "market" discipline it's not worth much – just a form of self-delusion.

Lessons from the Trenches

Where to look for advice on what to measure? In the abstract, IT only runs projects and delivers services.

For the former, there is plenty of guidance in the Project Management Institute as to what processes to follow, what they should look like, what should be managed and measured. So measures of cost, scope and schedule performance should be in place. The projects deliver assets (applications, middleware, infrastructure and so on) so once put into "production" these assets' availability for the client to use and responsiveness in delivering the capabilities the client needs should be measured on an ongoing basis.

For the latter, there is ample guidance in the Information Technology Infrastructure Library (ITIL). Again there is ample guidance as to what processes to follow, how they are to be defined, measured and managed. So services should be formally defined, including definitions of what constitutes "good" service as signed off by the clients who will be drawing on them. Delivery of these services should be measured as to their cost, elapsed time to successful completion and other parameters as negotiated with the appropriate clients.

At the end of the day, each organization will establish its own variations on what statistics should be gathered, what targets should be set and actual performance reported against them. Indeed, whatever is measured in the beginning should evolve over time in any case as old problems are solved and new ones come to light or are promoted. The challenge isn't so much in finding what to measure, but in how to prune measurements to a useful minimum and how to use them to maintain and improve performance.

The investment of time and effort into the measurement of the IT function's performance should in no way be treated as simply an academic exercise. It is a very serious business with an important purpose. That is for IT to hold itself transparently accountable to its client base, to face the music when performance is subpar, and to take concrete steps to continue to improve under all conditions.

Regular performance reports should be published or posted to intranet websites, or both. This is necessary but insufficient by itself.

In my view, IT best holds itself accountable in regular face-to-face meetings with clients. Whether weekly, monthly or quarterly, IT must openly and transparently present and discuss its performance for the immediate past – warts and all. The clients must have the opportunity to comment on the past period's results, to praise or complain, and IT should listen carefully and take action in prompt response when this is called for.

Moreover, while the IT staff responsible for whatever part of your operation is reporting must organize and prepare for these affairs, the IT leadership should regularly be in attendance. You must be there to feel the clients' pain and to experience their anger firsthand for your staff's shortcomings – real or imagined. (Trust me, often they are real shortcomings. Although almost equally often you may have a bad client who you must shelter your team from.) Some organizational cultures are more plainspoken than others, but it's always pretty clear when disappointment or frustration is being expressed. It's never pleasant to listen to it, but you must.

Quality like beauty may be in the eye of the beholder, but the beholder who matters in the case of measurement, and the quality of the IT team's performance, is the client. I firmly believe this, but I'm not alone, so kindly suspend disbelief and take it as a fact. Research the subject and learn, while your disbelief is beaten bloody and is ultimately banished.

Always take client disappointment like a (wo)man, and never get into a debate as to the veracity of the complaints. The last thing you want to do is to exacerbate emotions. Keep the dialogue open. Take down the facts and promise swift action to remedy the situation.

Time enough to gather facts and get to root causes offline when there's a better chance for all concerned to be dispassionate. Never play the blame game, or even think of hanging your staff out to dry, even if you believe they may well be at fault in some way. Remember, you're the one who gets "the big bucks" and who needs to get the work done on an ongoing and improving basis. Finally, remember who delegated the work to these particular staff in the first place and consider that the odds are better than even that the root cause of the issue can only be resolved by the person to be found under your tie. One way or another it's in your power to fix the problem. So do it.

And be sure to keep your promises of swift action. Report personally to the disappointed or complaining client within a short time of the meeting. Keep updating them – personally – until the situation is made right.

Once IT's clientele accept that the CIO and her/his direct reports take performance and accountability seriously, and will tolerate no BS or glossing over the facts, then the basis for a trusting, professional relationship between IT and its clients is in place. Mordac is in exile. Your job is to keep him exiled.

Delegation

As the CIO of an enterprise to which information technology is a strategic function you will doubtless be a manager of managers. So to be successful, delegation is a management concept you must master.

Just as an aside, it should become abundantly clear to you while reading this section on delegation, that with good IT performance measurement in place, delegation of your responsibilities to a team of subordinates can be relatively straightforward.

When delegating, you retain accountability for the work delegated to the manager reporting to you. You should expect and encourage this manager to take independent actions and make decisions within the scope of work you have delegated. So your mutual challenge is to work out the boundaries of the relationship, including the relevant performance measures and status reporting required, such that you are comfortable that the work is being performed properly, while your manager feels fully accountable for the subset of the scope of work you have delegated ("passed down" is an illustrative phrase for both of you to keep in mind). The importance of the key measurements to both you and to your delegate is that they define "goodness" for both of you. That leaves you both free to focus your interactions productively on exceptional situations and mutually understood roadblocks where collaboration between the two of you is necessary.

If you delegate too loosely (sometimes called "dump truck delegation") you essentially abdicate your accountability for actions and decisions taken by your subordinate. If some part of the work done by your manager turns out poorly, or is incomplete, you will only find out after the disaster happens. This is probably not good for your subordinate (and remember that you shouldn't be pushing her or him under the bus in these or any other circumstances). It certainly is not good for you, if for no other reason than it will be embarrassingly clear to everyone that you are not in control of the situation. If you are accountable, then you should know what is happening and why. You don't need to know every detail. After all, why have a direct report doing the thinking and doing for you, if that's the case? But certainly you need to know in general how things are going and what things are happening.

The tendency to go to the other extreme (sometimes called "micromanagement") turns your subordinate into a supernumerary – a figurehead – while you retain control of all details. This is not good for your subordinate, because s/he learns nothing from the experience of "managing" an area that you can't let go of. It also isn't good for you since you're still doing the work. As Mike Brophy, the Vice-President of Human Resources and my inimitable colleague at The Globe and Mail, once said: "Why buy a dog, if you're going to bark for it?" (There will be at least one more "Brophyism" later in this book, so be warned.)

Poor IT managers commonly resist proper delegation, using deflection and passive resistance to avoid actively working with their superior and colleagues to establish the boundaries of the relationship and key performance indicators of their role. A tell-tale symptom is poor and infrequent information about the workings of their "shop," delivered inconsistently or only when specifically requested. The question you have to ask yourself is this: if this person is so unwilling to be open with you – the boss – about what's happening in his/her shop, how open and communicative are they with their own subordinates and with their clients? Teach that person quickly that that kind of behaviour is career-limiting and definitely anti-team. If s/he won't learn the lesson, you have no choice but to remove that person. Or suffer the consequences yourself.

There are two additional reasons why you as the CIO must be very good at delegation.

First, your direct reports – the IT leadership team – are probably "managers of managers" themselves. This is true of all IT organizations of any size. So you have to be good enough at it yourself to provide an example and understand it well enough to coach your subordinates in the art and science of delegation. Otherwise, your management team will not be as capable as it can be – and very likely you'll fail.

Second, you very likely now have, or in the very near future will have, outsourced some significant part of the IT function to one or more outside vendors. You may not be thinking of it in terms of delegation, but in an outsourcing contract, you as the CIO are delegating some part of the IT function to be managed by a third party. The difference between delegating to an outsourcer rather than one of your direct reports is that your best opportunity to work out the boundaries of the relationship and mutually understood indicators that the work is being performed well, is before the contract is signed. After that, you have far less flexibility with an outsourcer than you will ever have with a direct report. There are obviously more complex forces at work in an outsourcing contract with a vendor than with an employee whose career is dependent upon your review of his/her performance. But I believe there are more similarities than differences.

More about outsourcing later. Finally, to close out this section, I have one brief story on delegation.

At de Havilland, some two or three years into my tenure as the CIO, we had reorganized the IT department along customer lines. That is, each of a number of managers reporting to me had responsibility for a "VP area." So there was a Manager of Engineering Computing, one of Manufacturing Computing and so on. Each of these managers was responsible for the relationship with each customer within their scope, and they had sufficient staff to run projects and support installed infrastructure for that customer. Shared infrastructure and services were run by a Manager of IT Operations who also reported to me, and was expected to treat each of the other managers as his customers.

Lessons from the Trenches

I had been continuing my plant walkabouts and had come to know many of the manufacturing and engineering management and staff quite well. I also continued my hands-on problem-solving as part of these walkabouts – something I rather enjoyed, and which greatly improved IT's standing with our colleagues in the rest of the enterprise.

One day I got an early morning visit from the new Relationship Manager in charge of manufacturing (let's call him Jack). We exchanged early morning pleasantries and sipped our first coffees of the day. Before too long, Jack started quizzing me on my recent interactions with people on the manufacturing floor. He zeroed in on a couple of small problems that had been brought to my attention and that I had had fixed. Finally he asked me why I hadn't included him in the interaction.

I hemmed and hawed something about time, and taking immediate action. I was beginning to feel uneasy for reasons I couldn't quite account for. He just smiled and suggested that since I had only recently put him in charge of the area, perhaps I should give him a chance to properly run it. His proposal to me was to change nothing in my wandering habits, but when a concern was brought to my attention, could I please ask: "Have you spoken to Jack about this?" If not, then I should direct him to do so (and give Jack a head's up so he could follow up). If the individual had done so, and no action had resulted after a reasonable time, then I should act.

Jack had me dead to rights, and provided me with a great delegation lesson. Before the reorganization, I had taken responsibility for the relationships with all VP areas. The reorganization along customer lines very explicitly delegated these relationships to my leadership team. However, until Jack called me on it, my behaviours had not changed – poor delegation.

Chapter 1 Basic truths

Celebrating success

In my sojourn in the trenches this is one fundamental, I freely admit, that I did not master. I think I fully understand its importance, and if I were to turn back the clock I would certainly invest more time in developing a comprehensive repertoire to do this well.

If you follow the guidelines in this book, as of course you will, you will enjoy success. Over time, your IT function will almost certainly improve its capabilities and focus. Project delivery will improve and operational effectiveness will improve. That's success.

Find ways to stop, recognize it and inspire your teams and your clients by sharing the moment. Have them join you to enjoy the vista from the higher place you have led them to. Too often we just start the next round of continuous improvement without a pause for properly celebrating the one we just successfully finished.

Ken Laver, my boss at two different periods of time at de Havilland – first as VP, Admin and later as CEO – wisely observed that both constructive criticism and praise are useful motivators. He also said that human nature being what it is, it seems that the former – finding flaws and offering advice on how to remedy them – is easier to do, so it's more frequently done. The trouble is that no matter how kindly meant and delivered, after a period of time the recipient starts to feel inadequate. The criticism starts to weigh on one's spirit despite the intellect's ready ability to accept the constructive part. So it has to be balanced by praise – by celebrating success – to even out the recipient's emotional books.

Ken's observation to many may seem like another example of the blindingly obvious. To me it was, and remains, a revelation. Once I'd heard him explain the psychology of it, I found many supporting examples of the phenomenon, and practical models to productively work with. One that I'll share with you is a book published in 1971 by Gerald Weinberg called "The Psychology of Computer

Programming." It applies Ken's observation (among many other useful ideas) to quality assurance within IT.

So I "got it," as I hope you have also. But I don't feel I ever "did it" as well as I should have done as an IT leader. The lesson on this topic ends here, with my advice to you to take more time than I did to learn how to celebrate success.

Chapter 1 Basic truths

Benchmarking

What exactly is a "benchmark"? In general, it is the comparison of something (anything, really) against a standard. In more usual business terms, it is the process of comparing some part or all of the enterprise's business processes, often to a peer group of organizations defined for the purpose and therefore used as the "standard" for comparison. The part of the enterprise, and its processes of interest here, is of course the IT function. What I am suggesting that we as CIOs would like to benchmark is the cost and quality of its delivery of its projects and services against that of a control group of IT functions in other enterprises.

Why would we want to do that? First, because it can be a major tool to foster continuous improvement. Second, and almost as importantly, is for your self-defence.

What's this about self-defence, you ask? The sad fact is that most people believe that they know more about IT than the IT department does. The equally sad fact is that sometimes they're quite correct. But what I'm concerned with here is the management of IT and of the cost and quality of delivering particular projects or services – in other words what should particular IT services delivered at a particular quality standard cost the enterprise? Without a benchmark to provide context as to who "out there" is actually managing to deliver the service at the desired standard, and what it costs them, we are all reduced to requesting heroism (in any case our clients will request it of us), and taking on the heroic role ourselves. Often without knowing it, we heroically try to be "holier than the Pope" – i.e. we try to deliver that which no one else, anywhere, has managed to achieve. Therefore we often stack the odds in favour of our own failure, out of ignorance and a misplaced "can do" attitude.

Can this be done? Of course. No matter what it is, someone has to be the first to set a new and higher standard of performance. Should you be trying to achieve this "best in all the world" performance for all your projects and services? Maybe not. But if you don't know that's what you're trying to do, what's stopping you? And what is preventing you from failing and thereby disappointing the rest of the enterprise that depends on you to do what you say you will do, when you say you will do it on a consistent basis. Do you imagine that will build trust for the CIO and his/her team?

Let me tell you two stories.

Avoid being "holier than the Pope"

At the time that I was hired as the CIO at de Havilland, it was a Boeing division. Boeing Commercial Aircraft Group had taken over the business from Canada's federal Department of Transport and over about five years had enjoyed considerable success selling de Havilland's products. But the de Havilland plant was unable to achieve quality of output and production rates to keep up to the order book. So Boeing was investing heavily to make the operation capable and therefore profitable. As part of that, there were heavy investments in IT. Soon afterward, for reasons too numerous to tell, Boeing put de Havilland up for sale, and shortly Bombardier acquired the company.

While Bombardier was organizing itself to integrate the operation into its other three aerospace acquisitions, de Havilland's business went into a tailspin. This was as a result of the double-whammy of a world-wide recession and of uncertainty on the part of air carriers just where Bombardier was going to take the turboprop commuter aircraft product lines of de Havilland. The important point is that due to the reduction in incoming cash flow, investment in many parts of the business dried up – including in IT. In fact, I was required to reduce budget and head count almost immediately after taking over as CIO.

Interestingly, business picked up for IT. My colleagues in the business while cutting their costs and staff, were looking to IT to help them to get more efficient and effective, so they wouldn't have to cut quite so much across the board. So while we in IT were cutting staff and reducing spending, we were taking on more workload. We managed to do more with less that first year.

The next fiscal year the downward business slide continued. Dash-8 sales continued to decline, and so layoffs and cost reductions were the order of the day across all of de Havilland. IT, like all other areas of the business, was expected to reduce costs by a company-wide fixed percentage. Once more we did so, and once more the IT "order book" grew for the same reasons as the previous year. We struggled to meet the growing demands on us, and along with the general emotional climate due to layoffs, the stress on the people in IT was considerable.

We were in an untenable position – in effect being required to be "holier than the Pope" and actually dying of "prosperity." I had to do something, but what?

An IT professional services company – Compass Analysis – had been trying to sell me on its services for about a year. Its name was based on a patented method it used to compare an IT client's performance to other IT departments in its database – both cost and quality – using a "compass rose." By using this graphical analogy, Compass was able to compare the client's performance both to the "average" and to the "top 10%." All in all, it was an elegant way of reporting and I was quite impressed. However, I had been reluctant to engage the company due to its cost and my concerns that we wouldn't necessarily compare favourably in the analysis. For all I knew, I might be required to cut more than IT's "fair share" and then we'd really be in a mess.

However, by the end of the second budget year of cost reductions, I didn't have much choice. So I consulted with the CEO, Ken Laver. Ken is intellectually quite a curious man and he was very interested both in their methodology and in the outcome. I got his support and we engaged Compass for the benchmark.

Some months later, the benchmark was completed and Dave Burkett of Compass made his presentation in our boardroom. There was a good turnout. The CEO was there, as were many of the Directors and VPs of the company. In the end, the de Havilland IT function was not found to be exceptional. We were certainly above average in performance, our costs were reasonable and so a step reduction such as was contemplated for the upcoming budget would be inappropriate (for which a sincere mop of my brow was in order).

We were found short of the mark, compared to the "top 10%" in a number of areas. Fortunately, part of the deal with Compass included a list of "best practices" that we weren't doing, but the top 10% were. So my mission became to put these best practices into place to move us toward a placement among the "best of the best."

Over time as we adopted these best practices, the IT function improved its economics and its delivery cycle times. As these were public and quantified, we gained a lot of credibility. We began to be budgeted differently than all the other functional areas. I and my management team were graded on our "rates" – or internal prices – for various services. Everything we delivered to our internal clients was charged out according to a fully burdened and user-friendly "rate" that was easily understood by the client and tied to services that were directly related to the client's activities. These had to be demonstrably "world class" at all times. A refresher benchmark was scheduled periodically to keep us honest.

Our clients, the senior management of the de Havilland division, had to tell us how many "units" of service they required from us in a fiscal year. The IT budget was calculated by multiplying rates times units and adding the whole thing up.

Was it as easy as it sounds? Of course not. Was it better than any of the alternatives? Absolutely.

So benchmark. I highly recommend it for CIO survival and prosperity. And for other, somewhat less worthy reasons.

Playing chicken with the outsourcer

Some years after the time of the de Havilland story, I took on the role of VP of Information Technology at The Globe and Mail, reporting to Roger Parkinson, the Publisher and CEO. This was a more exalted role for the CIO than it had been for "Canada's National Newspaper" ever in the past. Previous CIOs had been at the Director level, reporting to the Chief Financial Officer as peers of the Treasurer and Controller.

The Globe was very profitable in those days. It enjoyed what amounted to an advertising monopoly for an influential and wealthy market segment. At that time, if national advertisers wanted to reach a specific demographic (old white men with money), we were the only game there was. The revenue model at The Globe was 70% advertising and 30% circulation (sales of copies of the paper). Elsewhere in the print media, the ratio varied somewhat from newspaper to newspaper and from magazine to magazine but the basic model was essentially the same across North America. Since we had no serious competition for advertising to our core segment, money was just rolling in to The Globe.

Roger figured that others – competitors either current or potential – would see a good thing and would do their best to get in on it before long. So The Globe was organizing itself to take on any new competition when it arose, and to outperform it without breaking a sweat. The IT department would have a strategic role in that almost all the information systems used to create the daily newspaper and distribute it would have to be overhauled, made more flexible, adaptable, reliable and cheaper to operate.

This was going to be a tall order. Just a few years before, my immediate predecessor had been brought in to slash IT costs. (The business cycle had been at the other extreme and The Globe had been hemorrhaging money). He succeeded in doing so by reducing staff, economizing and by outsourcing large elements of the "raised floor."

However, a low-cost operation is not usually a flexible operation and rarely an operationally excellent one. I had a lot of changes to make and I would have to spend money. Roger was very supportive. I could spend all the money I needed – as long as I could find it in my own budget. Terrific.

I needed to redirect about a half million dollars of my annual budget. Doesn't sound like much, but the whole IT operating budget was only about $7 million to $8 million.

The biggest single budget item was the outsourcing fee, and the contract was coming up for renewal. I knew that the economics of IT outsourcing generally required the vendor to "buy the business" and run it at a loss in the first year or two. The vendor's strategy was to invest in automation to make possible the eventual provision of a constant level of service with fewer staff. By the last year or two of a five- to seven-year contract, the vendor would be enjoying a substantial margin. In our specific case, the vendor had delivered good service, and there was no need to change service level agreements (SLAs) or anything of the kind. Cutting the fee should be dead simple. That was my theory.

I immediately tested it with my account representative. No dice. He magnanimously offered instead to forgo any price increases for a multi-year extension.

So I did two things. I prepared to go to the open market for outsourcing services, and I called on the benchmarkers who had saved my bacon at Bombardier – Compass Analysis. I wanted some confirmation that my theory held water before I went to market and (possibly) made a fool of myself by having to actually pay higher outsourcing fees. After a few weeks of analysis, Compass came back with a "should cost" that would support a somewhat larger budgetary savings than I had been hoping for. Great – a margin for error existed.

Once more I had a conversation with my outsourcing account representative. I explained to him in general terms what the analysis had shown. Again, no dice. He commended me on my touching but naïve faith in IT benchmarking. Same offer was still on the table.

So I offered him a proposition that would remain open until The Globe's request for proposal (RFP) hit the street. If he would reduce his price by half a million a year, I would sign an updated contract extension for several years. Based on the "should cost" benchmark, I expected to save considerably more than that on the open market. But avoiding the hassle of transitioning to a new vendor was worth forgoing whatever additional savings there would be. However, once the RFP was on the street the proposition to him would be void, and I told him what day that that would happen.

I got a phone call on the morning of that very day, inviting me to an NHL hockey game that evening in the outsourcer's box. I was asked to bring my good pen with me.

Victory, thanks to benchmarking. (Of course I didn't sign at the game without a legal review. The account rep thought that as long as he had to give in, he could enjoy the drama of it all.)

Benchmarking summary

So once more I say, do benchmarking. Get objective, external and expert advice on what your operation should be costing the business for the levels of service it thinks it needs. It will save your career, and more importantly for the business, it will spare your valuable and vulnerable staff a lot of needless stress.

On an ongoing basis, it should also provide an ongoing source of practical continuous improvement ideas that will keep your IT team at the top of the game.

CHAPTER 2 MODELS OF IT MANAGEMENT

IT governance models

There are many of these, with the original models dating back to the early 1990s, arising from the early attempts to formalize the connections between corporate objectives and good IT management. Interest in IT governance received a very large boost after the corporate scandals around 2000 led to passage of the Sarbanes-Oxley Act in the U.S. and signing of the Basel II framework agreement in Europe. Then overall corporate governance – with IT an important subset – was top of mind worldwide. COBIT (Control Objectives for Information and related Technology) is probably the most popular IT governance model. It provides a reference model with the 34 IT processes typically found in an organization, and much detail about each of these "typical" processes for the benefit of those who wish to put good IT governance in place.

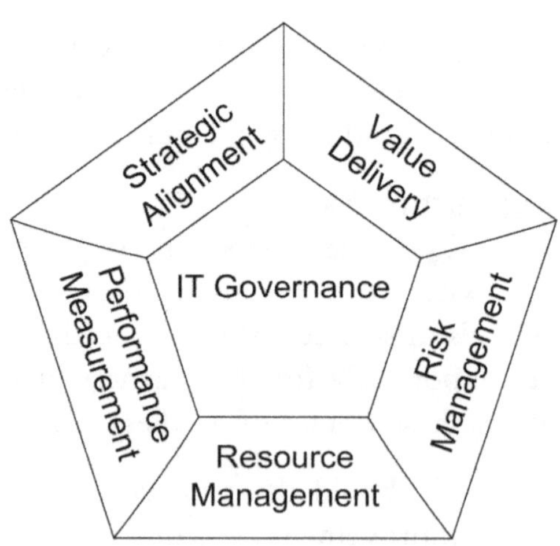

Figure 1 - COBIT 4.1 IT governance model

ISO 38500 also provides a framework for the governance of IT. It is even more complex than the COBIT model

These are mentioned for the benefit of readers – for two reasons. First, to make them aware of some of the many useful frameworks and bodies of knowledge that are available to them when they wish to formalize IT governance within their enterprise. Second, to illustrate that the proper management and governance of IT in an enterprise is no amateur undertaking. To do a comprehensive job of it requires the mastery of a lot of information in many important disciplines. And it takes a long time – several years – and a lot of effort by many people.

I suggest that no one should jump into COBIT or ISO38500 from a "zero base." It is too complex and confusing to do so. Training wheels are required. For this reason, I offer up the simple and practical model of IT management that is described briefly below, and further elaborated later in the book.

A simple and practical model of IT management

Much as the Project Management Institute has distilled the Project Management Book of Knowledge (PMBOK) into five process groups, and similarly the ITIL 3.0 standard has distilled IT service management into five process groups, I find it convenient to imagine an IT Management Book of Knowledge that is distilled into four process groups as depicted in the graphic below:

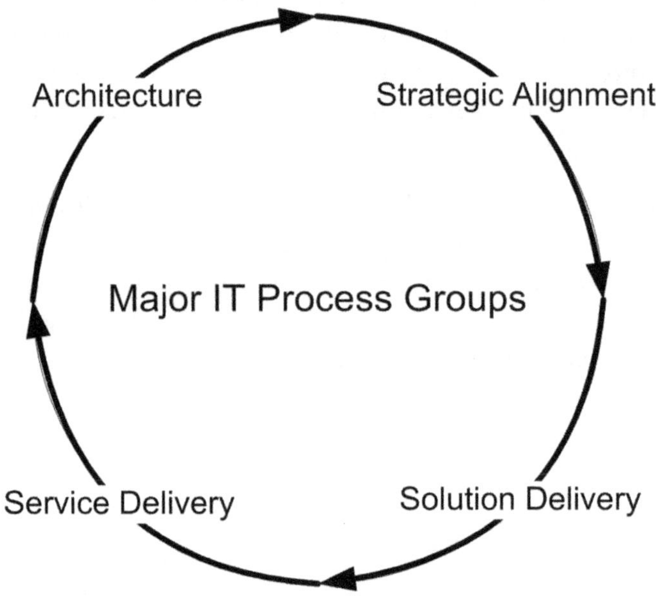

Figure 2 - A simple and practical model of IT governance

Strategic Alignment is the IT function whose purpose is to make sure that IT "does the right things," by putting an IT strategy in place that is capable of directly supporting the goals of the organization. The major input into this function is the enterprise strategy, the goals and objectives of the executives responsible for achieving it and the list of initiatives that these executives decide to pursue in order to achieve their goals and thereby their elements of the enterprise strategy.

One major output of these processes is a portfolio of capital projects ("solutions") to be delivered by IT, as prioritized and agreed by the business. Another is a portfolio of services ("services") to be developed and implemented for the business to augment the existing IT service catalogue.

The third and most important outcome of a worthwhile alignment exercise is to determine whether IT even has the structures, resources or skills to deliver what the business needs. Sometimes this means changing capacities of internal units. Often it means changing capabilities and outsourcing to acquire new capabilities as well.

These kinds of broad, sweeping changes are clearly not things that can be effected overnight, or even over the course of a single budget period. They are inherently multi-year undertakings for the management team of IT – time to put them in place, and time to confirm that they are indeed providing the capacities and capabilities originally envisioned. Therefore they are indeed strategic to IT, driven by the strategic requirements of the enterprise and must be explicitly aligned to its strategic plan.

IT must not only plan to "do the right things," it must have the agreement of the business that they are indeed "the right things." The agreement must be formal. It must be public, open and transparent.

Without these basics, the alignment of IT to the business at a strategic level is flawed.

Solution Delivery is the projects side of IT. It consists of business processes whose purpose is to make sure that IT is "doing things right" by implementing applications and systems that properly enable business capabilities. Input comes from Strategic Alignment.

The major output of these processes is the IT Project portfolio that will create new and unique IT assets that will be put into service to provide new business capabilities for business benefit. The proof of the pudding in this project portfolio is that each of the projects will clearly provide at least one key capability required for the enterprise to achieve its strategic goals.

Service Delivery is the operations side of IT. It consists of business processes that economically and reliably support all the systems and assets already implemented. It entails delivering all other services required by the business to continue deriving business value – as defined and quantified in the original business case – from IT investments that have already been made. Input similarly comes from Strategic Alignment. It especially requires careful attention to such matters as managing technical change so that things like routine software patching and deployment of upgrades don't screw up the systems and assets already in place. The proof of the pudding in this service portfolio is that they will insure that IT assets will consistently perform at levels required by the business to achieve its strategic goals.

Architecture is the design side of IT. It consists of long-range planning to put all the right elements of hardware, software, skills, process and organization in place over time —in such a way as to drive down the total cost of ownership of new and existing IT assets, and to drive up flexibility (reduced implementation time and risk) to implement new ones. Input comes from Strategic Alignment, and from real-life lessons learned in Solution Delivery and Service Delivery.

Other elements to the governance of IT certainly exist, and will not be addressed to any significant extent in this volume. Two glaring omissions from the model as discussed so far are IT security and mechanisms of accountability to the Board of Directors (Sarbanes-Oxley stuff). A careful examination of COBIT will indicate more omissions. These elements are not omitted because they are unimportant. They complicate the model and make it more difficult to understand the core mission of IT. Once the "training wheels" are mastered, it is incumbent upon the CIO to focus on incorporating these missing elements. It's unlikely that any CIO will ever be in a position to out and out ignore these other elements of IT governance, but to keep this book and its concepts easier to follow, I am setting aside discussion of these topics without in any way minimizing their importance.

These four major elements define a model for the management of IT– not the model. There are many others, that are also useful. However, this is the one that I am personally comfortable with and so I elaborate it in more detail, in the sections to follow.

Readers and practitioners are invited to adapt this model to their own enterprises, and to augment it as seems appropriate to their own situation.

Lessons from the Trenches

The need for a model

So why is a model of IT management necessary?

The flippant answer is that it provides a convenient framework for the rest of this book.

An only slightly less smart-alecky answer is that a comprehensive, consistent and comprehensible model of IT management provides some useful evidence to the doubters that it's not all BS and black art.

The proper answer is a more in-depth (and yes, more respectful) paraphrase of the second one.

A complete, integrated and understandable model of how IT is supposed to work is a useful tool for clients and for the IT staff. Tasks and goals that are delegated down the chain will now have a context. People will understand better what they are doing, why they're doing it and for whom. They can be more effective. True and informed empowerment of all the professionals in the IT organization is made possible.

In the same way, it is a useful tool for the clients of IT, the CIO's peers and colleagues. Understanding the model (being even aware of the existence of such a thing, in fact) makes them aware of the IT "ecosystem." They can proactively participate in the improvement of the ecosystem (strategic and operational planning, budgeting and business cases, etc.) and to ground their expectations of what IT can deliver, how they can or should participate in that delivery and how they can provide effective feedback on how well it's being executed. They can be enlisted to help improve IT's capabilities to meet their needs. Collaboration becomes easier and more focused.

In the upcoming discussions of each of the process groups, I set out what the entry criteria and the exit criteria (i.e. required inputs, expected outputs, and some other stuff) should be, and how IT management ought to go about making it happen.

Chapter 2 Models of IT management

If the reader will take a quick look back at the graphic of the "simple and practical model of IT," you will note that it is circular, implying a feedback loop; and the boundary between process groups is denoted by an arrow implying inputs or at least some form of progression from one process group to its adjoining one. At the top is "Strategic Alignment" and as has already been indicated, this IT function informs the others with input. It seems logical to start there, but we won't. We'll end there after discussing Solution Delivery, Service Delivery and then Architecture in turn. The thinking is that armed with the context, concepts and terminology of the three delivery process groups, we will be able to discuss Alignment more easily and with more clarity at the end of the discussion of the model.

CHAPTER 3 SOLUTION DELIVERY

Solution Delivery is the IT functional area in our "simple and practical" model of IT management that is concerned with the successful management of IT projects and the delivery of the "solutions" that such projects are intended to provide.

Why give it a different name than, say, "Project Delivery"? In many ways it would keep the terminology simpler. However, the intent is to emphasize that IT's role is not simply to complete a project. The finished product of the project must be a satisfactory solution to the problem or opportunity the business has tasked IT to deliver. The emphasis on solution rather than just the project is to emphasize IT's responsibility to be involved in the achievement of the right outcome as well as in simply following the management process.

The purpose of Solution Delivery is "to do things right." The "things" that have to be done right are to deliver a strategic solution as a shared responsibility between IT and its client, the business. That is: successful completion of one of the greater organization's strategic initiatives – those requiring new investment in IT systems and applications in order to make it possible for the enterprise to deliver the business results expected in its strategic plan. So the concept of "solution" as being the IT delivery objective throughout the life cycle of an IT project should be emphasized to everyone involved. It is important to keep this rather indirect relationship between the means that IT delivers and the responsibility of the business to actually achieve the committed business outcomes by using those means, uppermost in one's mind.

Hence I am sticking to the term Solution Delivery for this part of the IT function. While it's by no means a standardized name, the term is not original with me nor is it used only by me. I'm sure I picked it up from other people and I continue to hear it in IT governance discussions with other CIOs. (I'm guessing Meta Group likely were the big sponsors of the term before they were taken over by Gartner Inc. in 2005. But echoes of the term definitely still can be heard in CIO forums and other places.)

Annual capital budget and IT project portfolio

Generally speaking, the annual IT project portfolio is established by the enterprise capital budget. How much an enterprise can invest in total capital is determined by the cash flow it can spare to finance these investments. There is generally an upper limit to the total available capital envelope that is determined by the enterprise's finances and cash available. Naturally, in most enterprises not all capital is dedicated to IT, so the IT capital budget is some subset of the total capital envelope.

Not all IT projects can be capitalized. In particular, projects that plan to externally host the solution to be delivered (e.g. software as a service or web projects) rarely meet the definition of "capital." So the IT project portfolio typically includes a number of projects that must be financed outside the capital budget.

In practice, financing is rarely a constraining factor. The upper limit of the financing available for the IT project portfolio often is not reached due to other limitations. One of these is weaker-than-expected business cases for some of the projects that may have been originally considered for the IT project portfolio. Another is insufficient resources in IT and in the business to effectively initiate, plan and otherwise take the project to a successful close. A third, rarely addressed even in the most sophisticated enterprises, is "too much change" to one or more employee groups in the enterprise – thereby ensuring that one or more of the planned initiatives will fail due to "change fatigue" in the affected parts of the organization.

These Solution Delivery concerns, and some others, will be addressed more fully in the section on Strategic Alignment.

Chapter 3 Solution Delivery

Success criteria

A useful guide to the success criteria for an IT project is to look at a series of the Standish Group's Chaos Reports regarding the necessary success factors for large IT projects. Then make sure they're all in place. These have varied somewhat over the years, but the constants seem to be: executive commitment, user involvement, and good people on the project.

From the CIO's perspective (this one's anyway), it largely boils down to engaging a properly qualified Project Manager and thoroughly supporting him/her during the entire course of the project. A "properly qualified" Project Manager's duties (and therefore by implication his/her skills and capabilities) are spelled out in some detail in the balance of this section on Solution Delivery. In summary however, the Project Manager must be a strong manager to whom the responsibility for the entire project can be delegated (see the earlier section on delegation), from its initiation through to its closing. (An illustrative graphic providing a summary of the Project Manager's responsibilities appears at the very end of this section.) After having delegated responsibility for managing this project to this person, the CIO should be able to sleep at night; if not, then the wrong person has been entrusted with the job.

Engagement of the project's sponsorship and of the business resources required should also be explicitly spelled out as the Project Manager's responsibility. The IT leadership should be prepared to collaborate strongly to make sure that the proper engagement occurs subject to the leadership of the Project Manager.

Finally, the CIO and the rest of the IT leadership should make it clear to the Project Manager and his/her colleagues what is expected of them at various stages of the project. This requires a well-articulated and well documented gating process that defines how an IT project is to progress at the enterprise, providing what deliverables at what gates, from its initiation through to its closure.

If these guidelines are in place and care is taken that they are followed, then the enterprise can be sure to greatly exceed the "Standish average" for successful projects.

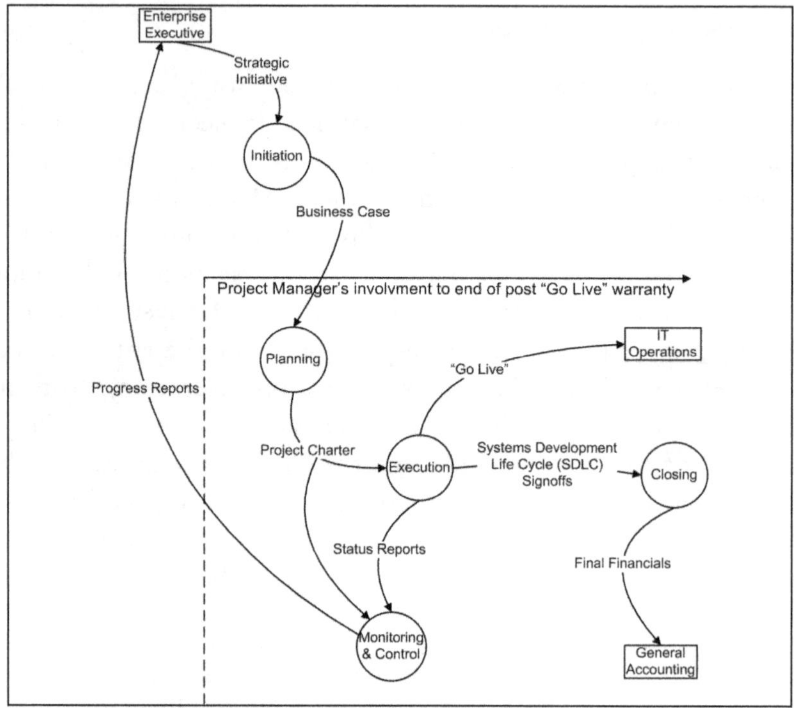

Figure 3 - Project Manager's involvement in gating process

Project gating process

Each individual project that is at the core of the Solution Delivery processes is governed (or in any case, it should be) by means of the five process groups of the PMBOK – initiation, planning, execution, monitoring & control and closeout. This is shown in a simple form in the graphic immediately above. The enterprise determines what decision/approval gates to place between which process groups (or even within process groups) to manage the progression of a project from initiation through to closeout, and which management bodies within the enterprise should be constituted to provide oversight of the progression of projects through these approval gates.

Most enterprises have significant numbers of capital investment initiatives, many of which are outside of IT, so the governance bodies constituted to manage IT Solution Delivery tend to adapt and blend in to more general capital budget management processes. Somewhat uniquely for the IT project portfolio, and particularly for specific IT projects, governance must take into account the fact that IT projects deliver indirect, almost symbiotic benefits as discussed several times in earlier sections. The new technological features and functions have no value in and of themselves. The business value is created by the business client(s) who do business in new, more effective and more efficient ways by using the capabilities enabled by the IT features and functions delivered.

The CIO and her/his direct reports must keep this distinction clearly in mind. They and the IT function they lead are not directly responsible for delivering the business value resulting from an IT project implementation. They are also really not in a position to do so without interfering with someone else's accountability or even doing someone else's job. Such interference, when indulged in by senior IT management, provides one of the clearest illustrations of arrogance.

More junior IT management and the IT professionals in their teams must constantly have this fact of life clarified and reiterated by the IT leadership team to prevent an unwanted slide into Mordacism.

Chapter 3 Solution Delivery

Initiation – boundary between strategy and solution

Project initiation is the first of the PMI's five project management process groups. It's good policy to emphasize within the enterprise that a project is considered initiated (i.e. passes through the "initiation" gate) when its business case is approved and funded. For continued survival and even sanity, the CIO must emphasize that both must be true – approved and funded. Until both happen, we don't have a project. We have what we hope is a good idea looking for support.

This is an important distinction for enterprises that normally manage a substantial capital project portfolio. Since "cash is king," many organizations have to keep a careful eye on their cash outflows to capital projects. Many business cases that are worthy of investment can be "approved," but the cash spigot can't be turned on right away, so they aren't "funded" right away. Sometimes the delay between the two steps when cash is tight, or for other reasons, can be of a frustratingly long duration for advocates of the specific project.

At this stage, I hasten to emphasize that how this is "gated" by a particular enterprise – whether in one step, two, or more – is at the convenience of the enterprise. Enterprises establish approval gates at each step along the way from a project's official definition through to its official completion as they see fit and as makes sense for the decision processes and structures by which they manage their activities. There are many variations on a theme and indeed major departures from the stages that I will portray here. My intent here is to cover and share my experiences with major milestones in a project's life cycle, not to set out a prescribed project process any more than the PMBOK does.

In most enterprises ideas for IT projects seem to always be "in the air." There is generally no lack of them; not any lack of opportunities to spend money on more information technology.

Nor do I mean to imply that they tend to be foolish ideas. In one way or another (in my experience, anyway) these ideas usually represent an intelligent impulse to make some sort of improvement, somewhere in the enterprise. What is often quite hard to find is a clear tie between the potential technology investment and how it will be used to actually realize some part of the enterprise strategy.

Good business cases should be based on a firm commitment to such a tie. The executive requesting the IT investment is accountable for this commitment, although s/he may be delegating this responsibility to a manager within his/her organization. Essentially the commitment can be expressed thus: "If you give me the funding I am requesting for this IT project, I will deliver the business benefits promised in the business case." Without the personal commitment of the Executive Sponsor, there really is no business case.

This is not a generalization. I view it as a management law – a clear corollary of the Standish Chaos Report. That is, perennially IT projects have been seen to fail due to poor sponsorship. If the "owner" of a capital investment business case will not make the commitment to achieving it, what kind of sponsor is s/he?

What kind of project will it be without such support? In most cases, according to the Chaos Report, it will be a failed project.

If the IT project portfolio management process is working well, then the IT project we will be discussing in this section is a priority for the enterprise. It must be completed on time, within the approved budget and delivering the capabilities envisioned in the committed, approved and funded business case. If it fails to do any of these, then the enterprise will almost certainly fail to achieve some part of its overall strategy within the timeframe it has committed to the Board of Directors, or to the equivalent governing body of the enterprise.

No pressure.

Before I close on the topic of project initiation processes, I will expand somewhat on what I mean by a business case.

Business case

Fundamentally, a business case should be a shining example of "completed staff work." If the reader is unsure of what that is, s/he should google the phrase, or just flip to the section in the last chapter on "advanced topics," where there is a short discussion of the subject.

In brief, a subordinate follows the principles of completed staff work if s/he presents a clear and concise statement of a problem or an opportunity, with a comprehensive analysis of the options available to solve the problem or to take advantage of the opportunity (and the pros and cons of each option). The subordinate makes his/her recommendation, the rationale for the recommended option is provided, and the subordinate awaits his/her superior's decision. If the analysis has been done as well as it should have been, the superior may or may not accept the recommendation, but if not, will almost certainly be able to confidently pick one of the other options based on knowledge (or preferences) not normally available to the subordinate.

There are always at least two options – the recommendation and "do nothing." In the case of IT projects, there are often viable options in addition to these two that deliver more benefits or less, for more investment or less. A CIO can earn many times his/her annual compensation by encouraging better and more thorough analysis of options at the front end of the initiation process, and thus maximizing the chances of a "cheap and cheerful" low-risk solution, over some "bleeding edge" high tech approach. The high tech approach has its attractions for many junior staff (and not only those in IT) which is understandable for many psychological reasons. Far too often this enthusiasm unduly influences the approval process and saddles the enterprise with more risk than necessary.

Once the appropriate option is decided upon, the business case boils down to a document wherein a certain amount of investment (cost) is identified and authorized in return for concrete and specific returns (benefits) that are identified in various committed business outcomes (made possible by certain IT capabilities) by the business owners. Thus the business case can be said to define a "solution," and with that the Solution Delivery processes within IT can be said to begin.

These three topics – costs, benefits, and the solution that will make the benefits possible – are the minimum content of a project definition as it appears in the project portfolio (or should be, or no one will really understand what "project" is being spoken of at Alignment time or whether it's even a good idea). The difference between a project definition for purposes of the project portfolio, and a business case for purposes of launching a real-live IT project, is one of additional layers of detail but also of firmly established accountability and buy-in.

The business case document, and the process whereby it is compiled and authorized, are the means whereby the enterprise convinces itself that a "good idea" that appeared at one time in the project portfolio for consideration in some future fiscal year, has just been promoted to a "good investment" starting in the current fiscal year.

At the highest level of abstraction, a business case describes and quantifies the benefits of an investment and the cost required to achieve the benefits. A "good" business case exists when the arithmetic of the total benefits and total costs yields an acceptable return on investment, or internal rate of return. The "solid" business case is a "good" one that has Specific, Measurable, Agreed-upon, Relevant and Time-bound (SMART) benefits. Every business cost reduction and every business service improvement that will contribute to the benefit dollar total must be quantified as an improvement in the appropriate performance measure. It must have the wholehearted endorsement of the business manager responsible for the performance measure, who will now have it built into his/her personal performance goals and objectives.

In effect, each affected member of the management team (the business stakeholders) must feel that s/he is entering into a contract that states: "If, with this IT project, you deliver the capabilities that I require and have explicitly described, then I will achieve the business benefits to which I have committed." It also helps a great deal if they have some real "skin" in this game – for example, if their performance bonus is in some direct way dependent upon achievement of these very specific goals.

This is no academic exercise. It is a necessary step in rallying the business management team both intellectually and emotionally to the cause. They must all be very clear on what they must give to it, and what they will get from it.

The leadership and the drive for bringing a business case to fruition rests with the enterprise. A business champion, or business sponsor who is responsible for the strategic initiative that requires some IT investment is the person to drive this forward.

In order to avoid creeping Mordacism, at least one of the IT leadership team has been actively involved with this initiative from the time it became a cherished opportunity for someone in the business, and has continued to be supportive in the formulation of the business case. This individual provides support to the project champion, and possibly at a very early stage, if the senior IT manager is an effective one, s/he may even have motivated the business sponsor to champion this particular investment.

Ideally, the author of the business case would be a suitably senior manager in the business. As a practical matter, these individuals have a "day job" and usually are grateful for IT resources to do the work under their periodic guidance. From IT's point of view the ideal author would be the Project Manager (PM) who will have to deliver the project. More usually, it is the IT Business Analyst who had been involved with the initiative when it appeared on the Strategic Alignment agenda. In my view, it is good for the enterprise for IT to provide this "ghost writing" service. The challenge is to provide this service and become familiar with the investment need of the business without relieving the business of its responsibility to actually deliver the sponsor's committed benefits.

Regardless of who authors and who "ghost writes" this document, early on in its creation, it is wise for this senior IT manager to bring in the person IT feels would be the logical candidate to be the IT Project Manager.

This is a win-win-win. The IT leadership team member stays involved without doing a lot of "heavy lifting" which is now delegated to the prospective PM. The prospective PM gets familiar with both the players and the business background – many important aspects of which never get written down. The business players get a good look at the IT honcho that they will have to live with for the duration of the upcoming project – many months, and possibly years. Everyone gets a chance to work together and begin the important relationship- and team-building process at the best time – the project's initiation.

Just to dwell on this point a little longer, because it is very, very important for the ongoing well-being of IT. There are three other reasons why the PM should be involved at the time of the formulation of the business case.

First, the PM needs an opportunity to consider what s/he needs to know about how to resource and how to govern the project. This requires an understanding of who the stakeholders are, who the champions of change are, and what kinds of subject matter expert (SME) resources may be required to define the IT requirements clearly in sufficient detail for ultimate success. This and other information that will be useful at the time of writing the detailed project plan (project charter) and later actually running the project is best obtained this way – with the PM rubbing elbows with the rest of the project team.

Second, in IT's self-defence, the PM must make sure that a thorough and complete assessment of the IT costs to bring this project off is performed before final approval. This is just about the last chance to do a good job of it without appearing obstructionist (or just about as bad, incompetent, with a "bad surprise" in the IT costs, much later, creating the unwelcome opportunity to possibly invalidate the economics of the project).

Third, it is an opportunity for IT to help everyone secure project approval by being a team player – by being innovative with ways and means to deliver IT features and functions. In the development of most business cases, a "cost wall" is struck where it doesn't look like the project will fly because the benefits are too puny to justify the kind of spending that has been identified to make it work. In my experience – at least as far as the IT costs are concerned – there is often more than one way to skin a cat, and therefore to reduce at least part of the costs. The PM can be a hero on behalf of IT by finding one or more such doors or windows through the "cost wall."

Total cost of ownership (TCO)

As an assist to both these latter two reasons, it's important to have a complete and consistent checklist that captures all the costs – especially before trying to indulge in any cost heroics that turn out to be an embarrassing mirage. One example of such a checklist – appropriate to calculating the total cost of ownership of a cross-functional implementation such as an ERP or CRM – appears in the table below.

Item	Description	A. One-time costs	B. Ongoing costs
1	Software	Commercial off the shelf (COTS) licences	Support (break/fix) Maintenance (upgrades)
2	Hardware	Servers and storage Networks Specialized peripherals Client devices	Support (break/fix)
3	Professional Services	Information System: • Discovery • Process mapping • Software setup and configuration • Software customization • Interface building • Data conversion /consolidation/loading • User acceptance testing • Training material development • Training delivery • Production cut-over • Warranty period • Handover to Service Delivery Hardware: • Install development & testing facilities • Install production facilities • Manage testing & promotion processes	Info system: • Application support • App "click up" • Regression testing • Training Hardware: • Hosting • Managed services • Moves/adds /changes

Item	Description	A. One-time costs	B. Ongoing costs
4	Project management	Central control of all "build" resources	Central control of all "operate" resources
Total	Total cost of ownership (TCO) = sum of A + 5 x B	All one-time costs over the implementation	All new ongoing costs for about five years after the production cut-over.

Figure 4 - Total cost of ownership (TCO) checklist

This specific checklist is not important in the details. It is more important in its structure, and the thinking it should provoke on the part of IT folks and their clients alike to cover all the bases. A one-time purchase of some hardware or software almost always means there will be the ongoing need to pay for support (usually several flavours of it) on an ongoing basis. The purchase of professional services for implementation almost always means there will be a need to pay for related support services on an ongoing basis.

The stories of organizations that went ahead and purchased an expensive piece of software but left it on the shelf because they had not considered the need or money for server capacity, implementation services, maintenance, or even more elements than those, often sound too stupid to be true. They are not all apocryphal. I know of several such in health care, and I'm sure that there are similar skeletons buried in the closets of many other sectors.

Private sector folks should certainly not feel smug. I know of at least one small manufacturer that spent a fortune on a modern ERP system, only to skip staff training because no money had been budgeted for it. After implementation, guess whose staff then started tracking orders, inventory, production schedules and the like on their very own individually customized Excel spreadsheets? About $200,000 worth of software, hardware and professional services sat and gathered dust for a few years until they got a new CEO who brought in an IT management consultant (me) to find out what was wrong. It didn't cost a lot to restart the implementation and make the new GM a hero. But the years of lost business opportunity were worth more than the system cost in the first place.

Summary

The summary of the lesson for IT management in business case preparation is:

1. Get yourselves (and if possible your PM) involved early;
2. Have the PM or resources available to her/him make sure all sources of cost have been identified and reasonably estimated, but
3. Counter the impression that the PM is trying to "obstruct" the project by loading on costs, and
4. Do so by actively (and visibly) looking for significantly less expensive ways of getting the work done.

Once the enterprise figures out how to get sufficient business benefits out of the project not only to pay off the total cost of ownership but to also get the economic return on the investment well above the prevailing rate, and has the right people "sign in blood" that they will deliver specific detailed benefits, then the ball is passed firmly to IT to get the project past the next decision gate.

Even in most large IT organizations with extensive project management standards, there is a fair amount of latitude available to Project Managers in how they choose to organize their project charters and/or project plans and to execute/control them. In my experience this is a good thing when the PM is experienced and has a track record of success – not so good otherwise. The remainder of the section on Solution Delivery sets out the sorts of things that the IT leadership team should be looking for to ensure all IT projects are structured to transparently and traceably deliver what is required by the business case.

Planning – the devil in the details

Project planning is the second of the five PMI process groups.

Once we have an approved business case, then we have the first of the two requirements for a project to proceed – approval in principle. Funding, the second requirement, is best based on a satisfactory and thorough project plan, which is the purpose of this second process group.

Many organizations proceed to both approve and fund a project solely on the basis of an approved business case. In my experience, this is a risky practice, because it tends to undercut the discipline of a thorough planning exercise. In more than one organization rather optimistic business cases cost-wise or schedule-wise are approved and funded – usually without such planning discipline, or much formal IT participation. When the project request gets to IT for delivery, guess what happens?

So I strongly advocate that funding of an IT project be contingent upon an approved project plan – one that is developed subject to considerable discipline and rigour.

In some enterprises, the business case is not finalized until the project plan is completed and approved. This is a logical, but also an onerous requirement since a proper project charter (at least of the comprehensiveness and quality that I have in mind) requires several person-months of effort to produce. Since many business cases don't secure approval, this effort ends up being discarded – a waste of time and resources. On the other hand, the enterprise may find it useful for its own reasons to establish an additional off-ramp or decision gate, making business case funding contingent on a satisfactory project plan.

In any case, completion of the project planning phase requires approval of a comprehensive project plan, which I will call a project charter. The project charter is a document loosely defined in the PMBOK (by chapter headings – the 10 elements of a project plan), that is intended to provide a more detailed examination of the actual solution identified in the business case, how it will be delivered, and by whom. But it is not intended by the PMI to be prescriptive of what a project charter should look like in detail.

Harking back to the criteria for a project's success – one of them being the need for an experienced, skilled and knowledgeable Project Manager – if the Project Manager to whom you have delegated a project cannot produce a satisfactory project charter, along the lines described below, then you do not have the right person in charge. If you're the CIO, you're not sleeping at night.

Project charter

I make very little distinction between the project charter and the complete project plan. Other people do: there is often a good reason to have one or more intermediate approval gates and to produce intermediate planning documents within the planning process itself before proceeding to finalize a much more detailed project plan. The charter may be the ultimate document in this process (as I am assuming here), or it may only be some form of "fill in the blanks" template of relatively small importance. As this is not intended to be a handbook on project planning, I will avoid making this distinction here, and speak of the project charter and of the project plan interchangeably as the documents used to secure passage through the planning phase and into execution.

In my travels, I have noticed that the project charter as utilized by various enterprises has a wide range of rigour reflecting the wide range of approval gates that a document with that title is used for.

Ostensibly the project charter provides a plan of how the work will be done, and who will do it. But, as for the business case, the focus of the exercise is to secure the commitment of the appropriate people. For the business case, it is commitment to the benefits to be achieved at a fairly detailed level. For the project charter, it is commitment to the delivery of specific capabilities – features and functions – within the overall cost and time constraints of the original business case.

At the highest level of abstraction, a "good" project plan takes the original business case and develops it in more detail. The capabilities the business has identified as necessary in the business case are "drilled down" into specific business process changes, and the software features and functions that will make the process changes possible. The resources that will deliver these more detailed requirements are identified – whether internal or external, and whether some of them will be acquired by going to the market via a request for proposals from qualified vendors. The high level, "benchmark" costs of the business case are broken down into the specifics of what resources are assumed to be required to deliver the features and functions – for how long and at what cost. Timelines are established as to when they can be delivered, and who determines whether they have been delivered correctly.

The external (purchased) hardware, software and professional services selection(s) are best not made until the project charter has been completed and signed off. This is my opinion, and by no means is it universal. Many organizations don't accept this, and do not finalize their project plans until they have concluded agreements with their external vendor(s). They generally reason that until they have their vendors in place, committed to their costs and timelines and properly integrated into the implementation team, the overall plan can obviously only be generic and theoretical, unsupported as it is by vendor contracts and commitments.

I have no quarrel with this logic, particularly if the enterprise only plans a small number of IT projects in a given budget year. If the number of IT projects planned is much larger than that (say consistently at least about 10), then for the sake of efficient and effective procurement, the opportunity should be taken to build a project charter based largely on shrewd assumptions and experience, however theoretical that may seem, before going to market to "nail down" vendors' costs and schedules.

In any case, a project plan with formal commitment from all the delivery agents to their quality (of deliverables), cost and schedule obligations is the other side of a viable contract between the business stakeholders (owners of the business case), and the Project Manager and his/her team. It in effect says: "If you provide this IT project with the stated specific resources and budget, I (the PM) will deliver the capabilities that you require, within the stated schedule and the authorized contingency."

To put it another way: just as the process of developing the business case is required to get the whole-hearted buy-in of the management team, the project plan accomplishes the same thing with the technical team. It also provides a direct and clear translation between the desired business outcomes, and the new technical capabilities that will make them possible. The common language that is most successfully used to accomplish this is business process.

When speaking of "the technical team," I make no distinction between internal IT professional resources, external contractors / consultants providing individual contributions, or external vendors providing significant subsets of the total solution. In most projects of any substance, it is not unusual to acquire IT resources both internally and from many external sources.

Before wrapping up this section about planning, we will briefly consider a few key concepts of the project plan/charter.

Goals, objectives and performance measures

Most project charter templates have a section with a similar title. This is a useful method of relating the business case benefits to be delivered to the implementation specifics of the planned project. It provides a handy mechanism to "delegate" the achievement of the business case to the various elements of the technical team tasked with delivering the various capabilities necessary to achieve them.

Each of the benefits of the business case can be stated as a goal for the project. Objectives are then stated as specific deliverables to be provided by the project in order to meet a particular goal (i.e. there would typically be multiple objectives or deliverables required to achieve a given benefit or goal).

Performance measures are then statements as to what "proves" that a particular objective is met or deliverable is completed.

While most project charter templates show only this three-level cascade –Goal→Objective→Performance Measure – there is no reason why it should be limited to only three. Multiple levels of objective can be used if required to show the relationship between benefits/goals, and the significant objectives/deliverables to be provided by a member of the project team. This is very much analogous to management performance measurement that progressively cascades enterprise management goals and objectives from the CEO's strategic goals and objectives down several levels in the management hierarchy. (Progressively, a higher level's objective is a lower level's goal.)

If you are reading this and are having trouble following the terminology and/or the logic, then please refresh your memory from your management training how delegation is achieved from one level of management to another. The concepts will be helpful here.

It's important to point out that the ability to communicate this part of the project charter in a way that is acceptable and understandable to all signatories to it – business sponsors, IT vendors, and internal IT staff – is absolutely necessary for all these parties to buy in. Think of this section as a kind of project management Rosetta stone, translating between several quite different disciplines and sets of terminology.

With all due respect to the tens of thousands of people by now who have achieved their PMP (Project Management Professional) certification – project management training is necessary but really insufficient to get this done properly. Some formal business management training and experience is also necessary – but even together with a PMP or equivalent, it is insufficient. The third necessary ingredient, which together with the other two provides sufficient knowledge and experience to clearly and concisely express project goals, objectives and performance measures, is hands-on IT technical experience.

The most valuable review point and most likely coaching opportunity for the Director of Solution Delivery and/or CIO to help develop more savvy PMs is here, in this section. Whatever else you do, review and provide quick feedback on this section. Help your PMs to get this done right, and the rest of the project charter more or less writes itself. (OK, maybe not all that easy, but certainly a whole lot easier with this section properly set out.)

Risk analysis

A project plan features a careful analysis of deliverables, costs and timelines, but also performs a formal and thorough risk analysis. Mitigation strategies for each identified risk (and their potential costs and timelines) are developed, and where appropriate, they are actually built into the budget and schedule of the base plan. Where not appropriate to build specific mitigations into the costs and timelines of the base plan for a particular risk, a scientific basis for an overall project contingency (both in schedule and in budget) for a set risks, is created – e.g. the proverbial "10%."

A capable Project Manager does a good job of identifying, explaining and planning mitigation of project risks. Like the saying about art, you'll "know it when you see it." It will be tied strongly into the specifics of the given project in ways that will make sense, which is something that is difficult to do by someone unfamiliar with the details of the project's subject matter and definitely tough to do by a Project Manager who has not encountered and later reflected upon, similar risky situations in his/her experience.

A rather generic risk analysis from your Project Manager – if this person is not able to visualize and articulate credible risks before the project gets underway – should be sending you serious warning signals about his/her ability to successfully bring the project home if it gets into difficulties.

Business requirements

A fairly detailed statement of the requirements to be met by the finished product of the project is indispensable to its ultimate success. It is required as input to a number of other key documents that are used as a means of communicating with key players in the project delivery process. Examples of these are: to provide to Solution Architects to help them scope the initial cost estimates; to provide to Procurement to create the RFP and to give prospective vendors responding to it a clear indication as to what the client wants so they can bid on it intelligently; to provide to Testing Strategists so that they can prepare test plans that can be used to objectively confirm whether the final product meets the stated requirements and is therefore acceptable to the client.

It is unfortunate, but perhaps unavoidable that business requirements tend to be developed parallel to, and sometimes outside of the business case and project charter disciplines. However, I have observed many useful and helpful results when the requirements document is related directly to the "goals and objectives" of the project charter (which in turn bases them on the capabilities required to deliver the business case). In other words, the specific and very detailed items – including features and functions – that appear in the formal business requirements can be presented as a more detailed "drill down" of an additional level, or two or three, of the "goals and objectives" of the project charter.

The approach of relating requirements directly to project goals and business case benefits, and maintaining visibility of those connections greatly aids something called "requirements traceability." This is a business analysis discipline (taught by the

International Institute for Business Analysis, or IIBA, and leading to the CBAP, or Certified Business Analysis Professional designation) that makes it possible to support the client (and technical team) in making decisions at each major step of the systems development life cycle (SDLC), which often at least by implication change the scope to be delivered. Doing a consistent job on the requirements traceability matrix greatly minimizes the misunderstandings as to the nature of the solution actually delivered at the end of the project – those when the client, amidst profound frustration and gnashing of teeth, finds out too late that one or more key requirements have been missed.

The formal terminology and methodology of requirements traceability is relatively new in my experience. However, it has been around as a technique for some time, even if only formalized as a best practice by the IIBA in the past few years. In fact, reflecting back on projects that I delivered in my consulting career, I can think of at least two where the teams that I worked with applied forms of requirements traceability with great success. These were at the re-engineering of all business processes at Enbridge Services around the turn of the century (God, saying that makes me feel old!) and during the implementation of a major supply chain ERP system for the Central Ontario Healthcare Procurement Alliance (COHPA) in 2008-2009.

Enbridge Services Inc.

In the case of Enbridge Services, we categorized all requirements as being in support of specific goals and objectives of the project charter (actually program charter, but I won't complicate things further by using the term – there were lots of large and related projects tied together by a "program charter" in this instance). The reason we did this was because the project was very large and complex, involving about 1,000 distinct requirements.

The business process re-engineering was driven in part by the need to simplify the technical environment, which involved the removal of some existing software packages and meeting the transformational requirements by the retention of a subset of them. Since many of the software packages were ERP-like in scale, the impact on requirements and therefore business capabilities of the wrong choice could have been disastrous. So the ability to assess whether the choice of one package or another would better serve the project's goals proved to be very helpful.

The Enbridge Services process re-engineering project was a complete success (although not right away – but that's too long a story for this space).

Central Ontario Healthcare Procurement Alliance

In the case of COHPA, the technical team was assembled after the hospital-specific ERP was selected by the business. COHPA is a shared services organization (SSO) providing "procure to pay" shared services to a consortium of six Ontario hospitals, which govern the SSO through a Board of Directors. The software package selection had to be made early to take advantage of time-limited funding, and a then-available consensus of the relevant hospital staff.

At the time the decision was made, the SSO formally had no more than two employees, including the CEO. The contract had already been signed with the ERP provider for both software and professional services, so there was very little additional leverage that the technical team could bring to bear.

However, the contract made progress payments contingent on "acceptance" at each of the hospitals making up the consortium governing the SSO. So we build a project charter that set out a requirements cascade starting with the goals and objectives, and built each hospital's user acceptance test (UAT) on that structure. We required each hospital to sign off on the project charter and the UAT test scenarios thus developed, which they did when they were comfortable with the UAT outcomes.

The ERP vendor wasn't entirely happy with this approach, as it had its own heart-felt ideas about what requirements were important and how to implement them, based on its substantial experience in implementing multi-hospital corporations in the U.S., so naturally there were some arguments. The hospitals and Board of Directors backed us as a result of our pre-work with the requirements.

All ended well. COHPA was the first Ontario healthcare SSO to meet its business case, and continues to thrive in its mandate, as of this writing.

Resources required

The project charter should specify who is going to do what part of the project's work. It is the PM's role to compile the project's dramatis personae, including past, current and future players.

This is particularly important if a substantial amount of the work will be externally purchased via one or more requests for proposal. The PM's thinking regarding how the scope of work should be packaged for one or more external vendors should be explained in the resources section of the project charter, reviewed and agreed upon by all relevant parties. This establishes the basic content of the RFP that is to go to market. The requirements, appropriately segmented by vendor as they are to be engaged, would constitute most of the rest.

All the other resources should be listed, and if possible at this stage, they should be named. Until they are named, the PM should consider the possibility that s/he won't get a required resource on board in time as a project risk and report it as such to his/her governance bodies. Examples of such resources are: subject matter experts from the business who will be required for (among other things) detailed process definition, signing off on detailed test scenarios, performing test scenarios, being trained and providing "expert user" support after the project goes live; architects to vet all the design work and possibly to do some themselves; business analysts to maintain the requirements traceability matrix and support the testers; one or more test managers who will prepare the detailed test plans and get client approval for them and will compile and report results at each stage of testing to the project governing bodies; and Service Delivery staff who should be tracking the project's progress toward operational readiness to satisfy themselves that all the requirements for ongoing support to the correct standard are being met.

These resources are an indicative list, not at all an exhaustive one. Specific projects will have variations on this theme. It should go without saying that who does the work and whether those people are committed to the project should be an early and urgent preoccupation of the PM. A fast way to get behind in your schedule is to have someone start late to do their share of the work.

Work breakdown structure and statements of work

It is useful to get into the discipline of getting all project resources, not just those from external vendors, to prepare a statement of work (SOW) which describes what deliverables they will produce, by what timeline, and at what cost. In a manner of speaking, the project charter is the sum total of all the SOWs of all the technical resources.

Each SOW should also make it clear who is responsible for accepting or signing off each of the deliverables provided under the SOW. (The best way to do this is through a RASCI chart, showing who is to be Responsible, Accountable, Support, Consulted and Informed.) It should go without saying (but amazingly far too often it doesn't) that proper segregation of responsibilities dictates that no member of the sub team providing deliverables under its SOW can ever sign off or accept any of its own deliverables.

Deliverables that are handed off from one technical sub team to another are signed off by the appropriate senior member of the receiving technical sub team – the one that is dependent on this intermediate result to create a deliverable for the end user. The most important deliverables will generally be signed off by a business stakeholder or her/his delegate. Regardless of who produces a deliverable per a given SOW – if it is handed off between two technical sub teams, or from a technical sub team to the end user – the SOW must specify who is responsible for signing it off to confirm that "Yes, it is acceptable."

One very powerful method for the PM to establish roles and responsibilities for each sub-team, especially external vendors, is to develop a work breakdown structure (WBS). For those with experience in manufacturing, it is very much like a structured "bill of material" of the final solution, made up of "sub-assemblies" of intermediate deliverables. Once properly prepared, the handoffs and signoffs should be clearly evident and who has to do what in what sequence (the "routing" equivalent, if you manufacturers are still with me) should be well defined.

A Project Manager who takes the time and effort to prepare a work breakdown structure for his/her project charter (with architects and business analysts sitting in on the process to help him/her) will have a much more useful planning document than one who just goes through the motions. I would go so far as to say that a well-structured WBS almost guarantees a successful project. Unfortunately far too few PMs are knowledgeable in the technique. A CIO and IT leadership team who want a consistently successful project portfolio will do their best to fix that.

Quality management/test planning

As alluded to in the section on statements of work, the RASCI chart is a necessity for quality management. An approved project charter or project plan, composed of one or more related SOWs, each with its own RASCI chart, sets out pretty clearly who is responsible for what major deliverables.

This is necessary, but not sufficient for a complete quality management plan. It essentially only covers the deliverables for which a subjective assessment of "adequacy" is possible. Ultimately, as more comprehensive subsets of the final solution to be delivered are completed, more concrete and objective means must be employed to confirm that it all “works as expected.” So a further requirement is a test plan or test strategy that allows for concrete and pre-determined means to confirm that it all “works.”

Even the simplest test plans have at least three levels or stages of testing. Often, there are more stages than this if the PM is concerned about the complexity of the solution, or its novelty, or has some other concerns about risk. We will limit our exposition to just the three “basic” levels of testing.

First, the owners of an SOW will need to perform “unit testing.” These tests take place in their own “sandbox” and are intended to show that what they will be delivering up the line to the next technical sub team actually works – at least in isolation. Generally these tests are for individual computer programs (e.g. for data loading, for customizations of a software package, or specific interfaces between new systems and legacy applications). The owner of the SOW allows for such testing in her/his timelines, but it is rare for the enterprise PM to build such detail into the solution’s timeline, unless there is some reason to doubt the capabilities of the specific team that a vendor has assigned to a particular project. (This is not, alas, a rare event. Even the most reputable professional services firms sometimes foist a “B” team on a client.)

Next comes “integration testing,” which combines two or more “units” under more controlled conditions than the “unit tests” and confirms that they “work as expected” when combined. Not infrequently, “units” that pass “unit testing” fail when combined with other elements. These failures are due to many reasons, one of the more common ones being differing interpretations of a specification or a requirement. Integration testing is usually the first real opportunity to “smoke out” such differences of opinion. Often enough, in retrospect one finds that the differing interpretations are each perfectly logical but are incompatible and cannot co-exist. So the PM is required to find some way to resolve the differences so that reprogramming and retesting can quickly occur, without impact to the schedule. If s/he is experienced and wise, s/he will involve all the relevant business subject matter experts (SMEs) in the decision.

Integration tests are built into the overall project plan's timeline, since they are a "gate" that can be passed only if the results are acceptance to the Accountable resource in the RASCI chart for the deliverable being tested. Therefore, they may not pass the gate on the first try (as noted above), so the timeline generally assumes at least a second try before this happens, with some time allowed in between for reprogramming and preparation for the second (or even third) try.

Finally comes the user acceptance test, which is conducted under the most controlled conditions of all, and which integrates all "units" to confirm that all the moving parts of the solution work together as expected. Unlike previous stages of testing, the UAT must be conducted by SMEs and/or casual users who will be expected to work within the new system once it "goes live." Otherwise, it follows much the same sequence as integration testing. That is, more than one try (or "cycle") is assumed in the project plan.

It is important to "work backwards" from defined UAT test cases in all integration and unit testing. That is, an appropriate subset of defined UAT test cases should be used for all testing. There are many benefits to this, not the least of which is forcing the early engagement of user/client SMEs in thinking about and preparing test cases. Since unit testing comes fairly early in any project, this means that at least a few test cases must be ready early (and progressively more must be developed at a steady rate as time goes on) or the project schedule will slip for want of test material.

The greatest benefit of engaging the client SMEs early in this way is that they are forced to think through at quite a detailed level just how the new system will be used by the various roles in the "to be" business processes. Their test cases have to use specific operational scenarios and specific sample data for several examples of each scenario, which further refines their thinking about how the requirements they specified for the system translate into operational detail. This is a very good thing for them to be doing while the technical team is in the process of building and integrating pieces of the overall system – and constantly in need of clarification of specifications and requirements.

Another big benefit is that the extent of testing is limited by the amount of time available to the SMEs to prepare (or to review and sign off) test cases without delaying the schedule. This can be a very large number of detailed tests indeed, and there is no implication that IT should play some kind of game to tie the hands of the business in any way. However, this definitely puts an upper limit on the number of test cases and tends to make the business focus on the highest risks and the highest priorities to test.

This put the onus for quality where it belongs – on the shoulders of the people who will have to deliver the business benefits once the solution is delivered. If some other approach is followed, then the onus tends to be on IT to "make it work" – a tough thing to do if the "target" is allowed to move.

I have dwelt on this (and could pound the point home at greater length) because of a hard lesson learned at The Globe and Mail – or rather not learned at The Globe and Mail. The pain of not setting up the test strategy as described above was experienced at The Globe. The lesson wasn't learned until a couple of years later at Enbridge Services, when I saw how it should be done.

User acceptance testing at The Globe and Mail

In the late 1990s, The Globe and Mail was enjoying a long string of successful and profitable years as Canada's National Newspaper. Executive management was pretty sure that this success would attract some direct competition, so a comprehensive strategy was put in place to make sure that The Globe would be able to outcompete anyone who dared to infringe on the franchise. Many of these initiatives required a lot of IT investment.

One of the key projects was to implement an integrated newspaper system. It was intended to replace a large number of old and inflexible systems that were used every day to put the paper together – to place and manage the editorial content, to flow the ads around it according to commitments made to advertising customers, to paginate and many other related functions.

The integrated newspaper system was to be implemented in several phases, including one that required the vendor to write a lot of new code. In those days (and even more so now) the market for newspaper software was quite small. Therefore the vendors were also rather small. Any project requiring any one of them to write a lot of new code was considered quite risky – not something one would "bet the business on."

At The Globe, we had no choice, so after a competitive RFP and suitable due diligence, we made a deal with one of these vendors. The first few phases of the implementation went well, until we got to the point where the new code had to be implemented. To mitigate the risks, an extensive UAT was put in place with exhaustive testing. Indeed, we hired external testing expertise to work with Globe employees to exercise the new part of the system.

Well, the testing was a great success. The new code was regularly "broken" and the project schedule started to slip badly. After a while the vendor began to complain about the excessive rigour of the testing (it was a fixed-price contract). Without conceding anything to the vendor, I began to question the testing and actually found myself asking whether some compromises could be made on some of the "defects" found. There was soul-searching on that point, but it was not felt that there could be any compromise. Testing must continue as it had begun and all "breakages" had to be fixed before acceptance would be granted. In the end, the vendor was fired and the rest of the project was abandoned.

It was only a couple of years later that I realized the total folly of the situation. With no basis for what constituted "passing" the tests established in advance (such as successfully processing "most" predefined scenarios and test cases), the exercise became a pursuit of perfection. Any defect found – no matter how convoluted the method chosen to "break" the code and force a software failure – meant a total failure of user acceptance. As everyone knows (or should know) any complex software system – and all the ones that have any business value are complex – inevitably have some "bugs" buried in them. So both the vendor (and The Globe's IT department) were faced with the hopeless task of eliminating them all.

Moreover, the onus was placed on IT and its chosen vendor to "prove that the system worked." It would have made more sense (as I subsequently learned in another complex project) to put the shoe on the other foot. Have the folks who had to use it when it was finished, define the tests to be carried out. In other words, put them in the position to "prove that the system didn't work" and that therefore the defects found were sufficiently serious that their business case could not be met and therefore they are the ones who must justify schedule delay and cost increases.

In retrospect, I am amazed that I was unable to diagnose the no-win situation we had placed ourselves into at The Globe and Mail.

Hence I dwell upon definition of a comprehensive test strategy in the project charter, on a UAT based entirely upon the "to be" business processes, and on test cases using real data approved and executed by the end users and their SMEs.

Assumptions

This section of the project charter can be one of the most useful, if the PM writing it is of sufficiently high calibre. The "assumptions" recorded in this section are a judgment call by the PM: they should be of a sufficiently high impact to the quality, cost or schedule of the project to warrant bringing to the attention of the project's sponsorship, and therefore documenting in their own special section of the project charter for later discussion at Steering Committee. The PM must also have thought ahead to the point in the project when a particular assumption will be borne out, or significantly contradicted, and should have even marked the point as a decision or review milestone in the schedule itself.

This explicit expression of assumptions and their potential impact on the project is another perspective on risk analysis. Its value is in providing another perspective to the PM on approaching this important set of management issues, and in providing the PM with a useful mechanism to manage the expectations of the project sponsorship (i.e. by providing the framework to help them understand that if otherwise "reasonable" assumptions don't pan out as expected, they may well have a serious issue to manage).

The best example that I can think of to illustrate the contents of the "assumptions" section of the project charter, is an assumption on a vendor's proposed price. You will recall that we are preparing the project charter for approval prior to going out to market to engage one or more vendors for some key project deliverables. A price has to be assumed based on history and experience. (This kind of project charter provides what in civil engineering is typically called a "Class B" estimate, where "Class B" is more or less defined as "ready to go to market.")

The quotes come back, and they turn out to be higher than expected – i.e. than explicitly "assumed" in the project charter. Now what? Well, now the PM reports the unpleasant fact at Steering Committee and work begins to resolve the issue. If the PM has flagged this as a key assumption and identified when and why it was to be discussed, the discussions typically take place in "solution mode" with all participants engage in a positive exercise to deal with an unsurprising happenstance. If none of this has been prepared beforehand, the Steering Committee feels surprised, possibly even ambushed, and thoughts of IT incompetence can be seen floating across their foreheads.

This is another bellwether of a good PM and a not-so-good one. If the PM preparing the project charter does a good job of the assumptions, s/he once again provides evidence to the CIO that s/he is worthy of being delegated the responsibility for an important project. Any other situation dumps the project problem into the lap of the CIO when the surprise comes, and the eyes of his/her peers turn laser-like to the CIO to whom, in all likelihood this is equally a surprise.

If you wish to be successful as a CIO, and a PM, to whom you have delegated the management of an important IT project, repeatedly exposes you to this form of embarrassment in front of your peers – not to mention showing so little foresight as to possible future events – either remove this person, or abandon all hope of being a successful CIO.

Execution – per the systems development life cycle

Once the project charter is signed off by all stakeholders, work actually begins on delivering the solution envisioned in the business case. At this time, two PMI process groups are underway simultaneously – project execution and project monitoring and control.

Project execution involves following the project plan, and creating the deliverables at the cost and at the times envisioned within it. For IT projects (as I prefer them to be managed), this means going into one or more procurement exercises, followed by another common methodology known as the systems development life cycle, or SDLC.

The IT project's execution phase adds some SDLC gates – Design, Build, Test, Train, and Go Live (or some close variant of these) – to provide some "granularity" to the single PMI milestone of "Execution." Each of these IT-specific gates provides a key deliverable to the ultimate solution. For success, each of these must of course be completed properly, and it is the Project Manager's responsibility to see that this all happens.

Design

In my experience, the key step in this process is design. A poor design almost guarantees failure. A good design provides the template whereby the overall solution's "Lego pieces" (often each produced to a different sub-team's design) fit together and move as they should.

Often the design must take into account past and future strategic considerations, so continuity in the team of Architects responsible for the overall design and the principles by which they work are musts. For these reasons, and probably some others, it is excellent practice to always maintain a strong team of Architects as an internal "design office." While it is feasible to outsource this function to an outside vendor with a good reputation for good technical design work, I don't recommend it for IT organizations that have an ongoing and substantial project portfolio (i.e. strategic IT organizations). Being strategic to the success of IT, this part of the Architecture function is best made up of career employees.

Build

The build phase requires the assembly of the various parts of the design into the functioning end solution. In the "old days" this often required a lot of custom computer programming to create a lot of the required features and functions. Today, due to the availability of a competitive and flexible market in "packaged solutions," this is rare. Be very wary of any technical team that recommends custom programming for any substantial functionality that is already available in packaged form on the open market. Sometimes these recommendations are based on highly optimistic cost estimates, and no consideration for total cost of ownership. Typically the "build" phase is literally an assembly operation, with some computer programming required to build unique interfaces between two or more purchased software packages. (Often even these interfaces have already been programmed with substantially the same characteristics as those called for in the requirements, and can be bought "off the shelf." In such a situation they are known as "connectors.")

Test and train

The testing process has been adequately covered within the project charter elements under "quality management/test planning."

Generally, the training process follows the successful completion of testing. The major reason for making training follow testing is to avoid training in functionality that is found not to work in the testing phase, requiring reprogramming to make it work, and very likely making it function in a different way than originally trained. Some overlap, to help compress the schedule or to create some schedule contingency, is always possible. But it's a risk.

Enbridge training team

At Enbridge Services Inc., while re-engineering all processes and systems right after their special-case Year 2000 fiasco, I saw one of the most intelligent ways to mitigate this risk. When there is some anxiety over the schedule, if the Project Manager needs to develop some schedule slack, an overlap between testing and training is simply unavoidable. (Yes, this is the same project where I finally learned about the correct way to set up and manage user acceptance testing.)

The HR department had a team of four or five who performed almost all in-house training. The standard modus operandi was to develop training material directly from UAT test scripts, using screen shots of actual test case outcomes with a minimum of filler. Work was started on the training manuals and on the reference manuals as the build phase was winding up, and the test phase was just getting underway.

Part of the team's "secret sauce" was its experience and continuity. That is, while small, it was large enough to manage some turnover without putting undue stress on the continuing team members to cope with the workload. It was also highly cross-trained so that almost any member's absence – whether temporary or permanent –could be covered by at least one other on the team. It was a knowledgeable hands-on group that to a limited extent could also cover for most of the company's administrative functions if required. In short, they were all masters of the business processes of Enbridge Services Inc. and they were personally expert in how these business processes were executed by means of the IT systems in place.

Due to this continuity and experience, they were able to assess the impact of particular UAT test cases failing, and not being repairable in any reasonable time. (There are a few of these in most projects – where the Project Manager has to push his/her technical teams to find workarounds. In the Enbridge Services business process re-engineering project, there were many of these, contributing over the UAT period to numerous "holes" in the originally planned set of training manuals.) So from personal experience and knowledge, they were able to prioritize the training materials that they had to rewrite to take account of bug fixes and workarounds, as they were developed by the rest of the project team. They also knew how to engage the Project Manager and other team resources to support their priority scheme, and to collaborate with the Test Manager and other test resources to get the revised material "hot off the presses," minimizing the amount of time required to update their training materials.

In short, this project's training materials were fully complete only a few weeks after UAT concluded, without any adverse impact on the aggressive training schedule.

Production cut-over/go live

After a successful UAT, and completion of training if it is decided that the solution is now "good enough" to put it into service, then the final SDLC phase is to shut down the old system (whether an IT system, a set of manual processes, or some combination) and to start up the new solution.

The illustrative term here is "cut-over." Often there is only a very brief period available (typically a weekend) during which business operations can be suspended, or in some way curtailed while the new system is "fired up" and put into service.

As most new IT systems introduce more information into business processes, the big challenge is to keep the old databases and the old data flows (interfaces mainly) from corrupting the new ones. Therefore a meticulous plan outlining all the necessary steps and their precise timing and order has to be developed by the project team, well before the intended cut-over date. Service Delivery folks have to be given the opportunity to vet this plan and satisfy themselves that the new solution will go into service without a "hiccup" (which ailment they will be on the hook to remedy once the system has been formally placed into production).

Work on this plan should be started as early as possible (once the design is finalized and approved), and it should be kept current with any changes that may result in the "as built" system due to deviations caused by UAT or other effects – as is the case for training materials. Typically these types of plans work on intervals of 15 minutes or less, for the two to three days of cut-over, and for several preparatory days beforehand and confirmatory days afterward.

I know all this stuff is rather dry. My apologies for being unable to provide an anecdote that describes a spectacular failure due to a poor job of planning and executing the cut-over. In all cases during my career, I have worked with teams who took this very seriously and we managed to get through it successfully. (Once or twice, we did have to abort the cut-over, restoring the old systems and data flows from backups. The cut-over had to be rescheduled, and eventually was properly completed. This is a delay, not a failure.)

For those who crave interesting times on their project (in the Chinese sense), by all means feel free to skimp on cut-over planning.

Monitoring and control – keeping it on track

Project monitoring and control involves tracking the progress against the plan, detecting deviations from plan, and steering the project back on track.

The Project Manager is responsible for both of these sets of activities, and of course if all goes according to the original plan from beginning to end, then there isn't much involved in project control, is there? Hands up all those who believe this ever happens – even once in a while.

Tracking progress

There are many ways to track the progress of a project, and probably most of them are quite satisfactory for most circumstances. However, the CIO and her/his leadership team should insist on a standard method to do this across the enterprise. The chief goal is to minimize the time wasted trying to understand a tower of Babel of different approaches to running all the IT projects under their purview. If your IT project portfolio is any more than even just a handful of projects, this is a serious management issue.

The work performed in reporting and tracking project progress is pure overhead. It adds no value to the project's final product. So the IT leadership team should also insist on a zero tolerance for "status BS" and wasted time creating status information. The best way to achieve this is to keep the method of reporting project status simple and unambiguous.

For most projects a "% complete" is useful, but only if the comparison is drawn between the "actual % complete" as of a given date vs. "planned % complete" as of the same date, as illustrated by the graph below:

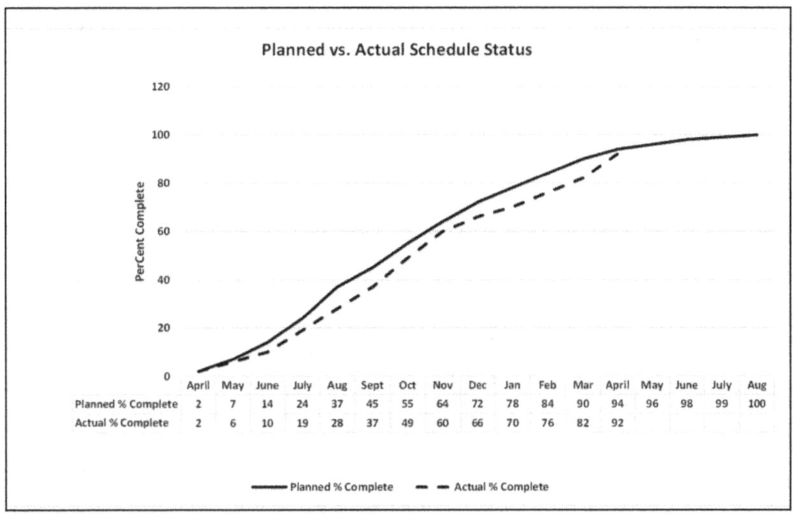

	April	May	June	July	Aug	Sept	Oct	Nov	Dec	Jan	Feb	Mar	April	May	June	July	Aug
Planned % Complete	2	7	14	24	37	45	55	64	72	78	84	90	94	96	98	99	100
Actual % Complete	2	6	10	19	28	37	49	60	66	70	76	82	92				

Figure 5 - Tracking project status by "earned value"

To avoid the confusion and inaccuracy arising from the "99% complete" syndrome (i.e. where a task is inevitably reported as 99% complete for a much longer period than 1% of its original duration), it is highly recommended that <u>only two values</u> be permitted for that status of a task. It is either 100% complete if it has been signed off by the Accountable acceptor. It is 0% complete until that happens.

Following this rule results in an "S-curve" with the characteristic of the one above – that is, the "actual % complete" curve is almost always below the "Planned % complete" curve, except on those rare occasions when it exactly matches. It is unlikely to ever be higher.

One of the significant benefits of insisting on the [0,100%] approach for task completion is that the gap is entirely accounted for by specific tasks that are not yet complete. By virtue of the RASCI chart, it is known who is Responsible for the tasks and their deliverables. The owners of these tasks are therefore on what may be colourfully (if impolitely) known as the "shit list."

The PM automatically starts the status review meeting off with a review of the "shit list." There is no reason to even talk about any other tasks or deliverables. If they were due, and completed, then what's to talk about? If they weren't yet due, then they aren't yet of interest, and so wouldn't factor into the "% complete" calculation until sometime in the future.

Far too often these meetings become an awful time waster, for which the PM must bear full responsibility. Project status meetings are for the PM's benefit, so s/he should have absolute control of the agenda, and s/he must take advantage of the face time with all other project resources to achieve his/her objectives of the meeting. It should be made clear by the IT leadership team that any other intrusions (i.e. "BS") will not be tolerated unless previously cleared by the PM and included explicitly in the meeting agenda.

The IT leadership team must continually remind the project team that "time is money" and a meeting attended (usually every week) by a large number of people multiplied by about one hour each of their time, makes for a very expensive meeting indeed. It should be productive and completely on topic. If the planned business is concluded ahead of time, then the meeting should end.

An amazingly accurate indicator of a PM's effectiveness, and of the respect accorded to her/his contribution to the project is provided by observing how directly and how efficiently the PM gains an accurate project status.

Risk and issue management

The reason IT Project Managers should be coached to drill right into the project's true status is because their time is best spent keeping projects on track, and there are plenty of pressures to push an IT project off course.

There are many interesting quotations from famous military men about the making of plans and how they don't survive much past the initial engagement with the enemy. My favourite comes from Dwight D. Eisenhower: "In preparing for battle I have always found that plans are useless, but planning is indispensable." The best illustration of that sentiment outside of warfare can be found in IT project risk management.

Project risks and project issues are closely related. Think of an issue as a risk that has actually happened. Similarly a risk is some event or result that would have a negative impact on project schedule, project costs or project deliverables – if it actually happened.

Generally speaking, the most common and most important risk assessment is made long before the project starts. The strategy to mitigate project risks is a vital part of the project charter's contents and of the overall project plan.

However, as the project progresses, some identified risks actually occur (i.e. become issues to be managed as per the mitigation strategy identified in the project plan), some identified risks become no longer possible nor relevant, and new ones become apparent. For this reason, some enterprises conduct a periodic review of current risks (sometimes also known as residual risks).

There are many ways to manage this phenomenon, but it is good practice for all projects to have a regular risk review. One fairly simple and painless way is to have project team members enter what they perceive to be new or important risks into a risk log. Periodically – say every four to five project status meetings – the PM puts a review of the status of the risk log onto the project status meeting's agenda.

There are more formal ways of doing this, but regardless of the method employed it is a good idea to keep an eye on evolving risk, especially for larger more expensive projects, and to maintain an up-to-date project risk assessment and strategies for mitigation of each risk, should it arise.

Issue management has to be more routine and continuous. A six- to 12-month IT project will generate literally hundreds of issues over its life, ranging from important ones that require several business executives to adjudicate, to relatively trivial ones that some project team members nonetheless feel are sufficiently significant to log, track and resolve.

Experienced, successful PMs always encourage project team members to raise issues. Indeed, quite often most of the issues that actually are logged have been raised by the PM. This is done based on the very sound philosophy: "If you don't know about a problem, you can't fix it. If you find out about it later, then it almost always has become a bigger problem than if you found it earlier." Better to spend a few minutes considering and resolving a fairly simple issue than having it grow into a monster.

The second hallmark of an effective PM (consistent avoidance of wasted time on BS status information being the first) is the characteristic lack of confusion or panic around her/his project.

All worthwhile projects generate issues to be resolved. They are unavoidable for a multitude of reasons. What is avoidable is for them to delay a project, to increase its costs and/or to impact its deliverables. All of them have the potential to do that, unless they are fielded, analyzed and resolved well before they can become a problem.

An effective PM runs a project that is quiet and unexciting because all the issues that arise are managed well before they become critical with no fuss, muss or unnecessary heroics.

Project Steering Committee

The Project Steering Committee exists to support the Project Manager in delivering a successful result. This may not be the conventional method of expressing its role, but it's the simple truth without embroidery. If that's not their main purpose, then what is?

The CIO and her/his leadership team should exert maximum influence to bring the enterprise around to this point of view. This section is intended to provide senior IT management with the rationale for this particular way of looking at Steering Committees and their role.

The Project Steering Committee has several specific responsibilities, but they all are subordinate to the "prime directive" outlined above. Why would a number of the senior management of the enterprise sit on a body designed to support a PM's successful delivery of an IT solution? The complete answer is because the PM is their agent, working on their collective behalf to deliver the means whereby they and their organizations within the enterprise can achieve the business case which justified the whole IT investment in the first place.

In my view, an IT Project Steering Committee's tasks are the following:

- To be the final arbiter in resolving project issues as they arise and as they are presented by the PM to the committee as a whole or to some subset of it, as is appropriate to the issue in question;
- To provide Subject Matter Expert resources from their own organizations as required by the project and as identified in the project charter. This role has the very important corollary of resolving priority conflicts within their own organizations either in favour of the project, or not. If not, then it is the responsibility of the Steering Committee member to justify to her/his colleagues the impact on the project – if any;
- To support, oversee, and sometimes to personally deliver messages of the communication plan and to oversee the management of the changes caused by the IT project; and
- To accept the final deliverables of the project according to the criteria pre-determined in the business case and the project charter.

The Steering Committee should be composed of a minimum number of players. The Chairman should be the Executive Sponsor in charge of the Strategic Initiative that is supported by this IT project. Given that we have assumed for the sake of exposition that most strategic initiatives are transformational and cross-functional, then members of the committee will be business sponsors from the other business functions requiring the capabilities to be delivered by the IT solution. All these players therefore have a specific and defined stake in the project's outcome. In an ideal world – which generally applies in the private sector, and very rarely in the public sector – these sponsors' performance bonuses are dependent on a successful outcome to the project. Moreover, they will also have a clear vision of what they expect to be delivered and so can be counted on to provide useful insight and direction when called upon to do so.

In short, the core of the Steering Committee should be composed of senior management who have "skin in the game." There are few situations where this will require more than three or four individuals.

Sometimes there is value in appointing functional executives who are responsible for providing significant resources to the project. In general this is done when these resources are not provided to the project under an enforceable commercial contract or its equivalent. This is most often the case in public sector projects where IT resources are assigned to a project under a toothless service-level agreement (or none at all), and there is no practical recourse for unresponsive service or poor performance. Providing a seat on the Project Steering Committee for the executive in charge of such a group under these circumstances is an attempt to introduce the resource providers to some accountability to the client. The hope is that if this executive attends Steering Committee meetings regularly, then Stockholm Syndrome will work its magic. Sometimes it works.

In my view the most important role of the Steering Committee is to provide a "supreme court" for issue resolution. The most important kinds of issues – by far – that arise in a cross-functional, transformational project have to do with the design and/or implementation of "to be" business process. Many of these can be quickly resolved by discussion with SMEs, but often enough the apparent alternatives available mean one group or another is presented with a bad solution – one that means higher cost, longer cycle time, or some other negative impact "for the greater good." When "kicked upstairs" to an ad hoc meeting of the affected members of the Steering Committee, a "sleeves rolled up" whiteboarding session comes up with a workable alternative that wasn't foreseen by the PM or the SMEs, and which doesn't require someone's ox to be gored. I have seen this happen often enough to have great and abiding faith in the value of an engaged Steering Committee of manageable size. (In any case, they ought to have the chance to earn their big bucks and their big bonuses!)

The Steering Committee's role of managing the assignment of their own staff as SMEs to the project is intended to manage a thorny and perennial issue for IT solution delivery projects. These resources typically are required for brief periods at widely separated intervals. It's very difficult to stay involved and engaged under these circumstances – particularly when these folks always also have a "day job." It's all very well to be striving to enable the business processes of the future, but the business of today has to be properly transacted for the enterprise to have any future. So these resources are very often caught between conflicting priorities. It's absolutely vital for the PM to be able to take these conflicting priorities to the appropriate Steering Committee member for resolution.

I will have more to say about change management (of which communication management is a prominent subset) in a subsequent chapter. Too often, enterprises and their executives naïvely believe that IT can "build it and they will come." Steering Committee members must be educated on their responsibility to prepare their organizations for the new way of doing business. It is in the interests of the IT leadership team and their PM to provide this education, and influence the Steering Committee members to take advantage of the time it takes to deliver the new IT solution to prepare their change management plans.

Lessons from the Trenches

There is no intrinsic business value in information technology. The relationship between an investment in information technology and the business value sought by the enterprise making the investment is indirect. The technology provides capabilities – features and functions – that enable the enterprise to do business in new and more profitable ways as the affected parts of the business see, understand and buy into them. A good IT leadership team will be sufficiently experienced and knowledgeable enough in the business of its enterprise to positively influence investment decisions, but will also be savvy enough to avoid arrogating the responsibility for imposing any part of a solution on the people responsible for its successful utilization.

Primarily for this reason, how the governance of an IT Solution Delivery project is structured and monitored – particularly a cross-functional one such as implementing ERP or CRM – is one of the crucial issues of IT management.

IT project closeout – closing ceremonies

A number of activities at the end of a project – after it successfully goes "live" – are bundled into the closing processes. PMI in its PMBOK does a thorough job of identifying and defining what these are. I will limit my comments to a few that I have found most important over my career.

First, and foremost is financial closeout. This involves expediting and paying all outstanding invoices, thus closing the books on the project and tallying its final costs by the appropriate budgetary categories. This must be done to satisfy both the finance department's needs for accurate asset accounting and depreciation, and the needs of the internal performance measurement function of the IT department, wherever it may report.

Optional, but highly recommended activities during this period are a quality review with the project's clients, and a lessons-learned session with all project participants. These are in effect the same activity, but differing by participants. They are both opportunities to take advantage of the great human teaching aids – what we did wrong (or at least not so well) and what we did right. This is best done in a brainstorming session with a good facilitator – one who can reliably keep him or herself emotionally uninvolved. The most important action for the CIO in all this is not particularly to participate in the sessions, but to be aware (and to be seen to be aware) of the proceedings of these sessions, and to quite visibly act on the feedback. There is no Solution Delivery shop that does its work so well that it can't be better.

Another optional, but very highly recommended project closing activity is the "victory celebration" – or the all-inclusive party for project participants to celebrate the success. For reasons that should be obvious, this should not be indulged in until after both the "lessons learned" and the element I am about to discuss – the project warranty – are completed.

Project warranty

This is not a term, nor a concept that I have come across anywhere else in writing, although it has often come up in discussions of projects that I have been involved with. The idea is a sound one, and probably should be made use of more often than it is. It seems appropriate to make it part of the discussion of "closing ceremonies" as chronologically the idea of a project warranty becomes relevant only after "go live," but it could just as logically be part of the project charter discussion as part of the project planning and resourcing. In any case, as it's never free of cost, it should certainly be accounted for in the project budget.

Very simply described, a "project warranty" is a commitment by the project team to remain in being and essentially at full strength for a period of time after the "go live" date. This is not done very often, because frankly it is a substantial expense to keep the project team in being for two to four weeks after the cut-over to production. Its purpose is as a form of insurance policy to reassure jittery clients that even if some key functional element or bug has been missed in UAT, that all the most knowledgeable and experienced resources will remain available to "jump" on it and to fix it as soon as possible. It is a mechanism to minimize the time to deal with post-implementation issues, real or imagined, so that confidence in the new system and new business processes does not become eroded – a genuine risk in situations where commitment to change is not whole-hearted.

If in doubt, then plan for a period of project warranty. In my career, often this has turned out to be an unnecessary expense in projects where the user acceptance testing was thorough enough to expose and remedy all the biggest quality issues – which these days is almost all of them. However, I have been involved in some cases where even a well-performed UAT proved inadequate, and having the project team available proved to be a godsend to the ultimate success of the project. Story follows.

COHPA initial hospital implementation

A great example of an instance where having the whole project team ready and able to support a system immediately after its implementation happened in 2009 at the Central Ontario Healthcare Procurement Alliance. The shared services organization for which I worked had committed to implement a modern and comprehensive "procure to pay" system for its six hospitals within two years of its formation. There were intermediate milestones, including the requirement to have two of the hospitals running on the new system within one year.

The decision was made to implement the first two hospitals essentially at once around April of 2009 – exactly 12 months after COHPA was established and started organizing its staff and the ERP implementation project.

All went relatively well. Some serious problems were unearthed during the UAT, but were resolved in plenty of time to meet the timelines for both hospitals. At COHPA, we were a bit nervous, since these were the first two hospitals, but were basically confident that all would be well. It wasn't.

It is a truism – often repeated to people who are new to system testing – that the best testing strategies and plans do not catch all the system problems. They only minimize the probability of serious problems still remaining in the system. The initial implementation at COHPA is a perfect example of this truism.

Soon after we went live, we discovered a serious bug in the ERP software, related to the synchronization of inventory counts taken on wireless handheld devices to the inventory database. Obviously, it hadn't been detected in the UAT or we wouldn't have gone live. It apparently had been in the vendor's software forever – no other client had ever used the system in quite the way we had chosen to do. So it had not been experienced, had remained under the vendor's radar, and arose out of this obscurity to plague the COHPA implementation. (This is what is called "pioneering"!)

In any case, the vendor had no immediate ideas on how or when it could be fixed. So consideration was given to delaying implementation until the bug fix was developed, applied and tested. The COHPA team and the hospitals chose to proceed, opting to use manual methods to compensate for the problem until it was repaired, rather than lose forward momentum. Elements of the project team, and of the COHPA staff provided the manual labour to compensate for improperly functioning handheld devices.

It took two stressful months, but finally the bug was fixed, and both the project team and COHPA staff could stand down. There was no further incident. The hospitals continued to use COHPA's "procure to pay" services thereafter with no extraneous excitement.

This was not, strictly speaking, a project warranty situation because the project team would have been kept together in any case. There were four more hospitals to implement over a period of another year. However, the team was still there and it was able to provide support in one of the few situations where a project warranty was truly required.

Chapter 3 Solution Delivery

Solution Delivery summary

It is called Solution Delivery, rather than something simpler like Projects or Project Delivery because it's useful to remind people of the obligation that IT has to actually deliver what the enterprise needs, relative to the enterprise strategy, rather than what it merely wants or thinks it needs.

The CIO's delegate in this instance is the IT PM, who must play an active leadership role in stewarding this initiative through successful delivery to ongoing support, where "successful" means that it meets the stated strategic needs of the enterprise, up to and including a realistic and ongoing 99.99% availability, if that's a business requirement, and agreed to be so in the business case.

To be successful, the CIO will pull out all the stops to support his/her Project Managers.

It is good practice for the same PM to be involved in all of the five stages of a project. To begin with, a good Project Manager, one beloved by his or her CIO, must have an excellent understanding of what the business is trying to achieve – the project business case.

Often this is problematic, since a project doesn't exist until it's initiated and usually that means an approved and funded business case. The enterprise doesn't usually start assigning a PM and staffing a project until that has happened, so the PM is sometimes reduced to reading to gain this understanding. An exceptional PM, one destined to gain the favour of the CIO, will find ways to get much more of an insight into what the Executive Sponsor and the other sponsors want to achieve, and will not proceed too far into the planning until s/he thoroughly understands it.

The most important piece of work ever produced by a PM is the "project charter." In my mind that's synonymous with the complete plan, whatever the form of the project charter template may be in any particular enterprise's gating process.

A good PM, one beloved by his or her CIO, fully understands Eisenhower's dictum about a plan – namely that it's worthless as soon as contact with the enemy is made, but that planning itself is very valuable. The project charter produced by such a PM therefore will not only have a well-articulated timeline, budget and scope; but it will also have an excellent and very specific risk analysis reflected in project contingencies; will have a rich and specific set of assumptions and will have clear and concise accountabilities assigned to all resources.

In short the PM and the project team will have already thought through how to adjust when, not if, things go wrong.

Once planning is completed, execution, monitoring and control start. A good PM provides unambiguous, no-BS status reports to the project's governance bodies. The "% complete" chart is just an example, but the key one.

It works best when only two values are possible for a scheduled task – 0% complete, or 100% complete. When the PM follows this rule in calculating the earned value curve, then s/he knows which uncompleted tasks account for the gap between planned and actual completion. And who owns them. A "shit list" is thus available, along with all the advantages appertaining thereto.

The corresponding financial chart can provide additional insight along similar lines. Accomplishments and upcoming deliverables come from the same place. Open issues are risks that have actually occurred (whether foreseen or otherwise). Current risks are a periodic update of the risks identified in the project charter. Some of them no longer apply and so vanish from the list, and some new ones may be added that arise as the project progresses.

Upon successful completion of execution, which must be defined by the client signing off on the results of the user acceptance test, the PM is ready to pull the trigger on the production cut-over. Thereafter follows an appropriate period of warranty. Once that is no longer required, then the PM proceeds to the closing out the project financials and the project lessons learned.

And that's Solution Delivery in a relatively small nutshell.

CHAPTER 4 SERVICE DELIVERY

Service Delivery is IT operations management – that is, the management of all IT assets that are in service (a.k.a. "in operation" or "in production"). That includes providing timely access to these assets, whether by providing access codes and passwords, hardware (such as PCs, laptops, cellphones and tablets), training in their use, and so forth.

Almost invariably going beyond this level, Service Delivery is presented and explained to the layperson in a very complex way. So that's why I prefer calling it "Service Delivery" rather than "Operations." Much as in the case of "Solution Delivery" vs. "Projects," the point is to make the mission clearer. "Operations" is certainly accurate but not really illuminating, and unlike "Service Delivery" (once explained) it does not focus on the purpose of the business functions gathered together under this heading.

This is a very important consideration because in fact, it is a very complex undertaking from many perspectives. The sheer number of items to be managed, even in a relatively small enterprise, can be overwhelming:

- PCs or other end user devices tend to average two or more for every person in the employ of the enterprise. (You don't believe me? Then count smartphones and tablets as well as PCs and laptops, and while you're at it include printers and scanners and specialty devices specific to various industries such as cash registers);
- The network tying them all together – both local and in the wide area – is made up of many discrete items of hardware and software to be managed and the "cable plant" – the physical wires that connect it all – is an important factor involving an enormous number of connections, all of which have to be managed. (Just think Richard III – "For want of a nail …");
- There is at least one server per application, and in fact usually there are multiple servers, whether virtual or physical; Not to

mention storage area networks (SANs), databases, websites, middleware, software applications and so on.

As a result of the sheer numbers of items to be managed, the Service Delivery function, more than any other aspect of IT, cries out for professional, down to earth, "by the numbers" management. If this isn't done well, then IT will not be a success, no matter where else it may do a good job.

Luckily, there's a comprehensive set of guidelines and management practices available – the Information Technology Infrastructure Library. This body of knowledge is comprehensive and well organized. The latest version, for the reader's reference, as of this writing is 3.0. It represents a substantially enhanced body of knowledge from the immediately prior version, and if a reader is familiar with 2.0. but not 3.0, it's worth your while to review it.

However, ITIL reflects the complexity of the subject matter to be managed – five core areas (service strategy, service design, service transition, service operation and continual service improvement), which in total encompass 26 IT processes, such as strategy generation, financial management, service catalogue management, supplier management, change management, incident management, and problem management.

And just to close out my harangue on "Service Delivery" vs. "Operations," note the prominence of the term "Service" in ITIL's vocabulary. I rest my case.

In short, there is a complex and comprehensive body of knowledge publicly available for the guidance of the CIO and his/her team. It is not the purpose of this publication to do anything more than to bring it to the readers' attention, to provide a soupçon of information about it, and to endorse its value for ongoing IT management.

Just as an aside, unlike the PMBOK, all the complexity and all the guidance within ITIL on how to deal with management issues is solely concerned with IT-specific management situations. So this body of knowledge is ours, all ours, and we in IT should cherish it far more than – in my experience – we do.

In any case, from the perspective of the enterprise, all that matters is how well the IT assets that are in service for the purpose of bringing business value are managed.

As noted above, there is a very large number of IT assets. However, most of them are there in a purely supportive role to the ones that matter. These are the IT systems, or applications which are the investments in IT that provide the capability to enterprise business staff to do their jobs "better, faster, cheaper." All the rest is a "bill of material" that is assembled into the final product of the performing application that actually enables business value.

Therefore the purpose of Service Delivery is to manage these applications – email, the websites, accounts receivable, order fulfilment, and others – so that they continue to perform as they were designed and delivered to do. Indeed, so that the enterprise derives the capabilities from them that it requires to achieve its mission.

How do you know Service Delivery is done well?

And more to the point, how can you convince first yourself, and then your clients, that this is the case?

The short answer is to measure and report the key metrics. Use the performance measurement to engage your clients, educate them in the complexities of the "IT numbers game," and provide constant and transparent feedback as to the ongoing performance of these assets and the technical teams entrusted with their optimal performance.

This requires a substantial investment in performance measurement, whether manual, automated or some appropriate blend of these. (Yes, I do hear the groans.)

So once our dear reader recovers from considering the tedium of gathering and managing dry statistics – for the purpose of holding oneself accountable, to add a forehead slap to the boring work – we will consider what to measure. What indeed? Actually, I gave it away in the previous section – application performance.

I can't put it any more clearly than David M. Fishman of Sun Microsystems in his 2000 paper "Application Availability: An Approach to Measurement," so I will quote freely:

"… Let's set a definition of availability as *continuous application access with predictable performance*. In daily life, this is fairly intuitive: call your travel agency, and you don't care whether the servers are up or down, whether the network is saturated or not, or whether the client application can validate your credit card data. To you, the only value of the system is in whether the agent can book your ticket or not, or how long it takes. The value of the service – and the service level metric that indicates whether that value is realized—is measured *at the end user's nose*. Naturally, to the user, the only measure of availability that matters is at the user – whether the user lives and breathes, or whether the user is some automated consumer of a service. In the online user world, that user's nose is a valuable spot: it represents the point where the application's value is highest – and usually becomes the most useful place to measure application availability …"

To me, and I hope to you also, this is indeed intuitive. Why the fuss and focus over the IT project that must deliver a "solution" – usually a new or upgraded application provided for the purpose of making the enterprise operate "faster, better, cheaper – if after the solution is delivered, IT does not take at least as much care in making sure it operates at the availability levels required by the business to carry out its strategic improvements?

So the starting point, the "boss measurement" that everything rolls up into, amounts to making sure that this is the case, all the time.

You may have noticed, that a number of important issues haven't been discussed.

For one, what is the target numerical value of the "… continuous application access with predictable performance …"? As most people know, this metric is expressed as a percentage of the time it needs to be available in a given period of time – usually a month. These days, applications are relatively bug-free and infrastructure is rock-solidly reliable, so that percentage values in the high 90s can be achieved without breaking a sweat. However, the difference between 95% availability (with useful performance) and 99.9999% availability could mean the difference between success and failure for the enterprise's IT investment business case. As we all in IT know, delivering the higher value could also mean huge differences in the cost of the solution that is delivered in order to build a system than can reliably meet the target metric. So it goes without saying that the target value that the business requires for this metric must be determined up front, in the business case.

When would you like to start to engage and educate your client on this particular metric? Or on what your brand-spanking newly delivered solution can actually achieve?

Hands up, all those in IT who know how to squeeze 99.9999% performance out of a system designed to achieve 95%. That would be pretty tough if not impossible. Being heroic and trying anyway would stress us out and make us look foolish. Luckily we in IT never place ourselves in such a no-win situation. Right?

Another way that this "boss metric" is viewed, is as minutes of unplanned downtime in a given period. Note that at 95% availability, a monthly total of more than 2,100 minutes of unplanned downtime is permitted; at 99% that shrinks to 432; at 99.9% it's just over 43 minutes; and at 99.99% this becomes four minutes. If you add any more "nines" to the uptime requirement, the number of minutes of downtime that can be tolerated drops below one.

You may wish to contemplate the implications for a minute or two, before we move on.

Managing target Service Delivery performance

You'll be pleased to learn that this requires more targets and more measurement.

Tracking and reporting on the availability of a particular application becomes a challenge in several ways (apart from the meticulous ongoing measurement of the metric itself). Just to pick two situations: what if your measurement shows that you're not achieving the set target, or it has somehow been determined that the enterprise would benefit from better application performance, such that a business case is being considered to invest in achieving said better performance?

How do you know what to do? In either case, you have to determine what to "fix."

That means you have to also measure the performance of the componentry that "goes into" the overall application's performance at "the user's nose." In other words, the performance of:

- the client hardware (PC, laptop, tablet or other equipment employed by the business user to get her/his work done with the application system we're focusing on);
- of the server(s) managing the application software;
- of the database server(s) or of the SAN; and
- of the network connecting them all.

The "technology stack" can be more complex than this, and frankly it usually is, but for the sake of this discussion I'll leave it at four relevant components to be managed.

I like to think of these measures as "diagnostics" in support of the "boss metric." IT as a whole is accountable to the enterprise, or at least to a particular application system's stakeholders, for the "boss" measure. The "diagnostic" measures help to isolate the problem – when there is one.

The target performance level of each and every one of the components must be at least as good as the "boss metric" target, or else the "boss" target will not be met. There will be times, for whatever reason, that the actual performance of one or more of these components will be below target.

As an illustration, refer to the figure below. It shows that target availability "at the user's nose" is 95%. It also shows the target availability of the application itself (i.e. the software that the user runs as opposed to the whole infrastructure required to deliver the application's service to her/him) has a target availability of 99%. So does the user's PC, the network, and the server. Wow, they all have a 99% target – overkill, right?

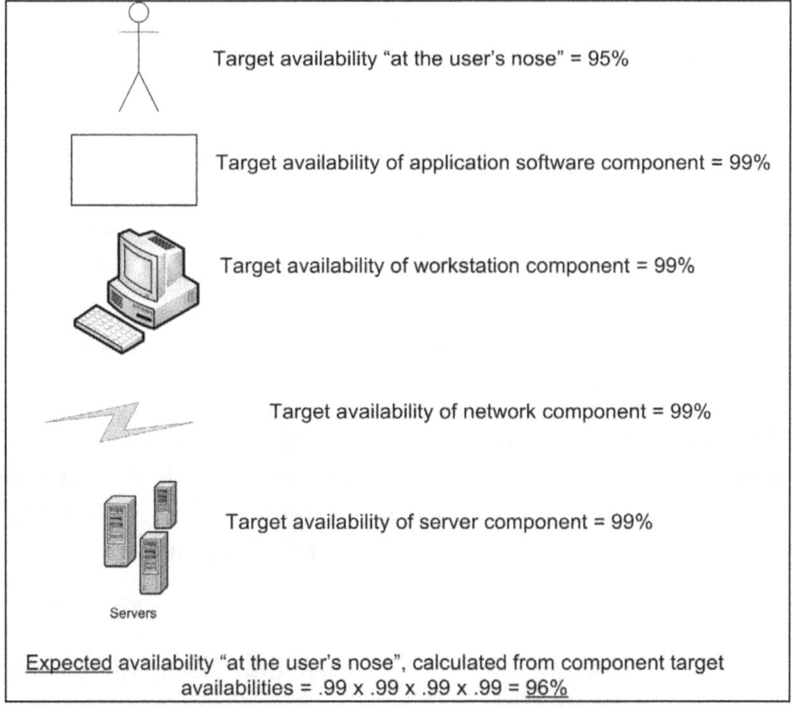

Figure 6 - Calculation of availability "at the user's nose"

Now, look at the calculation at the bottom of the figure.

How come we expect only a 96% availability with all those 99% targets? Probability theory provides the answer.

Each of the four components is independent of the others. So the probability of any particular component being available 90%, 95% or at its target of 99% has absolutely no dependence whatsoever on how any of the other components performs. So in that respect, predicting the availability of this configuration is very much the same as the old high school probability experiments, using coin tosses.

When you flip a coin, the odds of either a head or a tail are even. That is 50% each. Tossing one head has a probability of .5. Tossing two heads has a probability of .5 x .5 = .25. So if we equate "heads" to "available," and imagine tossing four coins (one for each of the four components) we see that the probability of tossing exactly four heads (all components "available") is only one in 16. Luckily "heads" in IT systems delivery (in this example) is .99 and we get a much more satisfactory result than 6%.

If your "boss" performance measure is below target, then look to the actual performance metrics of the components. One or more of them will have slipped below their target measure for the same period. Your task is to get the people responsible to explain why, and how they'll fix it.

If the goal is to re-engineer the "boss" target measure to be a more stringent one, then you simply go to the same people and ask them to explain how this can be done and how they'll do it. You might want to invite the Architecture folks to this discussion.

Easy, right?

Actually (for a change) there is no sarcasm intended here. It actually is quite easy. I don't minimize the effort in consistently collecting the statistics – whether manual or automated or some blend – and compiling them into the proper reporting. However, that does not require any intellectual leaps; it just requires diligence and professionalism. Then you manage with the facts at your disposal.

The alternative – failure to gather and transparently report these metrics to the enterprise – is a dismal one. Far too many IT operations teams shy away from doing this, and all of IT pays the price in diminished trust. More often in complete lack of trust, too much cynicism and acceptance that "Mordacism" is the norm.

I can't emphasize this enough. If you don't measure it, then you don't manage it. Worse, you will be seen by the people you're supposed to be serving as not holding yourself accountable; as not being worthy of their trust.

So to summarize: how do you manage target service delivery performance?

First, pick targets that mean something important to your clients. That invariably means some variant of application availability.

Second, report on the actual performance of these "boss" measures, and on the equivalent performance figures for the componentry that these top-level services are dependent on.

Third, be ready to explain root causes and remedies for any "bumps in the road" – temporary failures to meet the targets in actual terms.

Finally, be ready to propose long-term remedies that (usually with some focused investment) will permanently improve actual results. Your clients may or may not be interested in making such an investment at any given point in time, but it's in everybody's interest to be ready with a well-thought-out strategy and plan on the shelf for when it may be wanted or required.

It's a numbers game. Your clients have to be informed, educated and regularly reminded about the real issues and especially about the volumes involved – the number of assets IT has to manage, the number of incidents that these generate and the relative impact of each on service levels. Playing this numbers game really is much easier than any of the alternatives.

Chapter 4 Service Delivery

Engaging clients to achieve outstanding Service Delivery

There is no "one size fits all," entirely unlike the situation in Solution Delivery, where the Steering Committee made up of major stakeholders is the logical venue for engagement. In many organizations, a forum for operational reporting will already exist and IT simply has to work at conforming to it. It has been my experience that you often have to feel your way to set one (or more) up that works for everybody.

If there does not already exist an effective forum to discuss IT Service Delivery performance, you should definitely and proactively work at setting one up. The alternative of delaying until some crisis forces IT to come "cap in hand" in front of some tribunal of angry stakeholders to convince them that IT knows what it's doing, is a very poor one. (And if it isn't obvious to you that it is a "trial" in every sense of the word, then you haven't experienced a true IT operational meltdown that has impacted the enterprise. Or you weren't paying attention.) If you wait until then, you put IT into a deep hole that will take much energy and patience to dig out of, and will greatly impose on what remaining goodwill there may be among your clients.

An example

The best example from my experience that I can share with you comes from de Havilland – the Bombardier Aerospace division in Toronto that specializes in commuter turboprop aircraft – Dash-8s. Earlier in this volume I spoke of being persuaded, on my first day as the new CIO there, to do a lot of "managing by walking around" at the large plant site. The example I'm offering up here comes from a little later in my tenure. Please bear with me for a few paragraphs of context-setting.

Boeing Commercial Aircraft Group sold de Havilland to Bombardier Aerospace shortly after I was hired as de Havilland's CIO. Boeing's big challenge with de Havilland had been to get the plant and workforce to build aircraft fast enough to keep up with the order book. Boeing could sell aircraft faster than de Havilland could build and deliver them to paying customers – regional airlines.

This was a bigger challenge than it may sound. Commercial aircraft are generally not produced according to a "cookie cutter." While particular models have a lot of commonality, they also have a very high option content. Airlines insist on "their" modifications, and there are other sources of variation. Configuration control and quality control challenges are at least as difficult as in any other form of manufacturing.

To help solve the problem, Boeing had moved many of their managers up from Seattle to work with us, and they also hired an army of consultants from all over North America. These groups of bright and knowledgeable people had no lack of plausible ideas as to what had to be fixed and how it should be fixed. An elaborate portfolio of projects – many of them IT projects – was in place to support the recovery strategy. When Bombardier took over, all these consultants were let go and most of the Seattle managers returned home. Most of the projects were quietly shut down.

Instead, Bombardier asked one of the senior Boeing executives to stay on as COO for a couple of years to fix the problem. This was Jim Schwalm, a 25-year veteran of aircraft manufacturing operations at Boeing.

Jim's approach to solving the problem was to select a single "boss" performance measure that properly framed the problem, and then to make all management responsible for achieving the target. He chose parts "shortages" as the measure. Simply put, a "shortage" was defined as the lack of a part or item required for an assembly or sub-assembly when the manufacturing schedule called for it. The supervisor or manager who lacked the part and therefore could not proceed to meet his production schedule obligations as a result was the customer of the supervisor or manager who failed to provide it on time. The supplier "owned" the shortage, and was responsible for improving his process so that the rate of shortages he imposed on his customer(s) declined over time.

Each "owed" part corresponded to one shortage. At the time that Jim started focusing us on this measure, de Havilland had thousands of outstanding parts shortages at any given time.

Jim made it clear to everyone that he wasn't pretending that this was any sort of magic bullet. When the "shortages" problem was fixed, if the larger manufacturing rate problem still remained, de Havilland would pick a second "boss" performance measure and drive it in the desired direction. What Jim wanted was focus on resolving one and only one big problem, and to hold everyone accountable for its resolution.

One of the pointed signals that Jim sent regarding accountability was to hold meetings at 6 a.m. and at 6 p.m. every day, to be attended by all management whose total shortages exceeded a particular target level. We were an airframe manufacturer, so of course the morning meeting was ruefully referred to by some as "the dawn patrol." Naturally the evening meeting became the "sunset séance." Until a manufacturing manager's "boss" measure was at target or better, he had to spend at least 12 hours at work, not necessarily including time to prepare for dawn and dusk patrol. That target level kept being lowered over time, to keep the motivation for progress at a high level, and of course the ideal target is zero shortages.

Very early on in the proceedings, IT became the "star." "The shortage report is wrong/has a bug in it/etc." was the early, regular refrain. So of course the complaining manufacturing manager succeeded in deflecting his problem onto us and away from himself, thus sparing himself attendance at the dawn patrol and the sunset séance.

Jim invited me in to chat about this. I expressed the opinion that IT really wasn't the problem. Jim didn't think so either, but he wanted to manage the issue, not argue over it; to deal in facts, not opinions.

My instructions from Jim were gentle but very firm: be at those 6 a.m./p.m. meetings to deal with each and every complaint as it arose. Install a workstation in the boardroom so the investigation could be initiated right away, and with any luck also solved immediately. In any case, IT was expected to react immediately. He did believe that his management were raising smoke to avoid accountability, but that at least some of the time – probably in a minority of cases – they were actually right about an IT error or bug. In either case, IT had to expeditiously diagnose and resolve every reporting issue or complaint, or his campaign for focus and accountability would fail. And it would be Al's fault.

No pressure. We did as Jim asked. Of course, some real issues with shortage reporting and related data sources and application systems surfaced, but none turned out to be very serious. We fixed them quickly. Within weeks, the use of IT as a smokescreen stopped, focus was put on the real problems and the ship began to move in the right direction. Shortages declined in a matter of a few months from thousands monthly, to a few hundred and often fewer. This in fact, solved the overall business problem. There was no need to "promote number two" issue. De Havilland was once again able to successfully match its manufacturing rate to its sales rate.

For me, the whole experience was illuminating. When I started, I was told that at de Havilland IT had a bad reputation. These shortage reduction events happened not too long after that. The IT folks had been maligned by their colleagues and thrown under the bus for expediency's sake. But with the forum that Jim Schwalm had established, IT had managed to prove the calumnies wrong and to shift attention back to where it had belonged. And this had all been accomplished very simply. The IT folks merely did what they had always done – fixed problems in their systems, real or imagined – and all turned out well.

The difference, of course, was that we had been compelled by Jim to directly and publicly face what amounted to a series of challenges to the quality of service that we provided. He had simply applied the instincts and practices of manufacturing operations to IT operations. He also didn't care what the truth was, as long as it was discovered and shown to be in fact the truth. Each complaint was confronted in a factual way, and successfully dealt with, as a part of a problem-solving exercise.

My appetite had been whetted. I wanted IT to do more along the same lines. While I pondered how to go about this, internally within IT we started to measure our own performance according to what we ourselves felt was important. I made it clear to the rest of IT management that these reviews would cease to be purely internal very soon, and that we would be presenting the same performance statistics to our clients. The panic and fear among my team was surprisingly vehement and almost universal. It seemed to boil down to the widespread concern that our performance statistics would simply provide our clients (I sometimes felt that "our enemies" could be substituted without any loss of meaning) with additional ammunition to crucify us. I let people blow off steam, but also made it clear that I was adamant. We were going to publicly and in person present and discuss our performance in a client forum.

Meanwhile at Jim's instigation, or at least with his full support, de Havilland started slowly to publicly review its own performance in quite some detail. Over time, the dawn/dusk patrol meetings were no longer required. Instead monthly "quality/cost/schedule" (QCS) reviews were established. They started in manufacturing operations, but gradually support departments (such as facilities management and design engineering) were required to attend and report on issues which they owned which were impeding manufacturing performance. Over time, the contributions of support departments on specific issues brought to the surface by manufacturing, evolved to their own regular reporting on support metrics and projects of interest to the manufacturing audience.

Ultimately, these QCS reviews were established for all functional groups at de Havilland, and conducted by each Vice-President for his area. Performance against corporate goals and top performance measures was reported by the responsible management to their VP. Support departments (IT, human resources, facilities engineering and others that provided necessary services) were required to attend and report on their performance obligations in support of the achievement of these goals.

Much to the consternation of my direct reports and their teams, IT became a prominent player at all of these reviews. All of them got to face their clients and to defend their report card in public. This illustrated for me the general truism that everyone in the enterprise is IT's customer. The monthly meetings weren't anywhere near as traumatic as my colleagues feared. They all managed to live through them and did so quite successfully for many years, although at times of course we all had some very difficult things to report and explain. Also, I must say that the reputation of the IT department at de Havilland rose substantially as we become more involved with the QCS process. Complaints, rumours and slander of IT dropped to almost nothing.

What did we report? In most of these VP QCS forums, we started with the fairly comprehensive and complicated charts and statistics that we had started internally to report to ourselves. In all forums over time, by popular demand this was boiled down to essentially four sets of measures:

- Availability of key applications (to the corporate function – manufacturing cared about different applications that did engineering; customer support had its own set; and so on);
- Availability of key shared resources, such as the campus network and of the mainframe (which in those days ran a large share of the critical applications for many functions – especially finance);

- Timeliness of support response to incidents (i.e. average time to respond and resolve as well as % resolved within a few hours, a day and several days); and
- Status of projects compared to plan.

The middle two are actually related, and represent partial bellwethers of the first measure. I think it was well understood by our clients that the availability of shared resources, and the "timeliness" measure were both simply an input into the "availability" measures. But they seemed to want some insight into the underlying processes we used to maintain the availability of the application systems that were important to their own performance. And they also were interested in understanding how much of our best technical resources were consumed in support vs. in project work – looking for warning signs that a favourite project might be delayed because a key resource or two had to be redirected to fix an operational issue.

Was it an unqualified success? Yes.

How do I know? Well, I made mention a few paragraphs earlier of the greatly reduced "noise" about IT. There's no doubt in my mind that if we hadn't made ourselves publicly and transparently accountable to our clients in a very fact-based way, the noise levels would have continued high and IT's reputation would have remained low, as it had been for quite some time prior to my arrival on the scene. Moreover, these sessions became invaluable forums for all attendees to float ideas about future improvement. Many successful problem-solving and business case developing teams were initiated at these sessions. IT was asked to participate in many that had only a peripheral IT requirement. So, clearly we and our clients were thoroughly engaged with each other – something rather new at de Havilland at the time, and very desirable anywhere.

Other evidence? One time at an engineering department QCS, our engineering Relationship Manager reported a flawless report card. (And no, this didn't happen very often at any of the QCS forums).

All performance measures stood at or above target. A series of successful project deliveries were made in that particular month – several of them actually ahead of schedule. Dr. Fernando Cicci, who was the Director of Design at the time, was smiling, nodding his head and murmuring "good work" at each bit of good news. He had been one of the most outspoken critics of IT in the past – polite but pointed. I turned to him and asked: "So, what do you think of IT now?" He paused for a minute, and then finally said: "You're not as bad as all the others." (Meaning the back office functions such as HR and finance, about whom he had been equally critical in the past.)

Warms the heart doesn't it?

An approach

So, how can you make these good things happen to Service Delivery in your IT shop?

Well, as was mentioned early on in this Service Delivery section, you have to have measurement in place. You have to have handy the "boss" measure of application availability to which your clients will be able to relate and will moreover be able to intelligently discuss (and insist on your delivery of) targets rooted in their business needs. You also have to have "diagnostic" measures in place. These are useful to IT in understanding how the performance of the componentry is affecting the "boss" measure. Some of it (as in the de Havilland example) may also be of interest to your clients on at least a temporary basis, from time to time. In any case, IT certainly needs these diagnostic measures to stay on top of the "boss" performance measure.

I don't minimize the effort required to achieve a useful and self-consistent measurement regime. There's a lot of work involved in establishing an effective incident management process; an effective problem management process; an effective capacity management process; and many other of the ITIL-defined processes. Without most if not all of the 26 or so IT business processes that ITIL 3.0

speaks to, you will not have the data to produce reliable measurements. However, clearly most of this effort is not merely driven by the need to measure. It is required to establish an effective Service Delivery function. More than 90% of the effort is to make your team capable of "doing," while less than 10% is to make them capable of "measuring." In effect, the machine you build to do a proper job of Service Delivery (processes, organization, vendors) provides through its "exhaust," the data to measure its performance.

So in other words, the effort necessary to establish effective performance measurement in IT Service Delivery is pretty minor compared with the effort necessary to put in place the ways and means of actually doing the job properly. Why would you then be deterred from putting in performance measurement on the basis of "excessive effort"? Without measurement you would never know if the Service Delivery function you put all this effort into establishing is actually doing what it should. This would be tantamount to "swimming the ocean, only to crash on the beach" (the quotation is the second Brophyism I promised you earlier on).

The final ingredient to Service Delivery success is one or more regular means to engage your clients – face to face. You need to establish one or more regular forums where you and your clients have "sleeves-rolled-up" discussions about the performance of IT in the past, its impact on the business, and what needs to be changed in the future. I was very fortunate at de Havilland in that the culture already made monthly QCS mandatory. This made life for IT very much easier. In fact, very few enterprises in my experience, are as disciplined as the de Havilland organization was in those days. That's too bad, but in the absence of such an enterprise-wide performance management discipline, you have to find a way to achieve Engagement with your clients.

Clearly, there's no one size fits all. You'll have to adapt to the enterprise culture and develop a way to have these conversations with your clients that work best in your particular environment. It doesn't have to be the same methodology for all stakeholders. Your biggest clients (those parts of the enterprise most dependent on flawless IT Service Delivery) are the logical place to start since they have (or should have) the biggest need. If you can, approach some of your most outspoken critics with an offer to work together to improve things, starting with open and transparent measures of your own shop's performance. Encourage nature to take its course and evolve the format of the meetings and the reporting provided – guided by the ideas of those who take you up on your offer.

Option 1: the best approach is to start engaging your clients proactively.

Option 2: when a crisis hits. If your IT operations appear to have dropped the ball, before you manage to proactively establish regular Service Delivery engagement, immediately get in front of the crisis. As I've commented earlier in this section, this is not the best option. However, for heaven's sake, don't retreat into a shell until you feel you have perfect data, reports, approach etc. to deal with the situation. If IT is dragged into the limelight for negative reasons, such as a disaster event, waste no time dealing with it. Show your (the CIO's) face and face the music. Offer a diagnosis if you have it, and admit it if you don't yet have it. Deliver diagnosis and action when you have it, and status on a regular basis, even if much of the time there isn't much to report. You'll feel foolish and unprepared. You'll undoubtedly experience a lot of disappointment, frustration and even anger. Very likely you and your team deserve it. (As the head of your team, you get to "own" it. That comes with the big bucks.)

Be as humble and as professional as you can to manage through the current disaster. Openness and transparency at this time is the only approach that I've seen work. Build on it later, as circumstances permit to develop and evolve the relationship with the clients affected to get to a more positive place. If necessary, use it as the justification for regular, structured, performance checkpoints.

Managing the crisis in this way is nothing more than the IT version of the "customer service moment" that is experienced in many businesses. That is, a disappointed client is not a bad thing if you can work with the client in such a way as to convince him/her that you are sorry for the bad service, that you are willing to make things right, and that you care about the long-term relationship.

Option 3: is any other approach to engagement. Too often, I have seen IT get caught by a crisis before an engagement forum is in place. Remember, from the de Havilland example that usually means that IT is unknown, unappreciated and therefore due to its lack of visibility IT tends to have a poor reputation. Then, when caught this way, IT goes into a shell for a time to develop a "perfect" response. Meanwhile the crisis deepens and IT is seen to be missing in action. Does this dig your hole deeper? Yes, it does.

So, respecting approaches to establish client engagement Option 1 is the absolute best. Remember that you'll be racing the clock to prepare for it, as the inter-arrival time of IT crises is not very long, and never predictable. It's very likely you'll be presented with the opportunity for Option 2. Take it. Take advantage of whatever preparation you already had in place while you dreamed of an Option 1 scenario; have faith in your team's abilities and in your client's sense of teamwork and fair play; take your lumps and work hard to use the crisis as the basis for long-term engagement.

Option 3 is the wrong one. It appears here because sadly many IT Service Delivery functions react with Option 3 and end up written off by their clients.

Help desk/service desk

There are many teams and roles within Service Delivery, but the one that has the most frequent contact with the clientele is the "help desk" (more properly named the "service desk" in ITIL terminology).

This is the first, and single official point of contact for IT complaints (the "help" part), and requests (the "service" part). For that reasons, it is also often called "first level" support. While to the uninitiated it may seem like a simple, straightforward function, it really is not. In "the wild" it has a wide range of sophistication.

At the simplest, a help desk simply fields and records all calls from clients before passing them on to the relevant "second level" support or service team to deal with. This is popularly labelled a "catch and dispatch" service desk. Even at this simple level, the help desk is a valuable resource. If nothing else it imposes a necessary discipline on the client base. Many successful IT departments insist that if the call is not made to the help desk and recorded (the incident number provides proof of recording), then it never happened. "If we don't know about it, then we can't fix it" is the policy often enforced by Service Delivery units. Given that even relatively small enterprises record more than 1,000 incidents per month, there truly is no room for informality in reporting. This is often a bone of contention with stressed-out clients. If the policy is not enforced, then it's actually an even worse problem. But a socially acceptable approach is to occasionally log incidents on the client's behalf.

A more sophisticated service desk fields and records all incidents and requests, and resolves a high percentage of trouble calls right over the phone. The higher the number of incidents fixed on "first call," the more efficient the whole Service Delivery function is, and more importantly, the lower is the service time lost (a.k.a. "downtime") by the client. For this reason, this goal of an ever higher percentage of calls resolved at "first level" has for many years been a desirable best practice.

The most sophisticated service desk goes beyond simple fielding and recording of incidents and requests. It makes effective use of the wealth of information that is typically contained in the log. All service desks are expected to publish performance statistics about the desk's own speed of response and its effectiveness. The best desks also analyze the performance of "second level" and "third level" support teams, and recommend improvement strategies. Often, a service desk operating at this level of sophistication is outsourced to a particularly effective vendor, sometimes one that specializes in this function. Many outsourcing consultants recommend hiring firms that specialize in service desk and continuous improvement, on a gain-sharing basis. To avoid any question of conflict of interest, this particular vendor is generally not given any other outsourcing scope.

The help desk/service desk may not be the most important part of the Service Delivery organization, but it is "the face" of IT for most of its clientele, and the most important source of operating data. So this part of Service Delivery should always get special attention, and should be seen to always be operating at a very high standard of customer service.

Service Delivery challenges

From the CIO's point of view these fall into a couple of broad areas – cultural and managerial.

What I am calling cultural perhaps has a better label. In any case, I refer to the tendency of operations staff generally (not just IT operations staff) to resort almost excessively to "heroic" measures. That is, they seem to derive considerable satisfaction from working hard to resolve "incidents" and thereby save the day by averting or mitigating some sort of disaster – or appear to. Suspicion starts to arise when the near-disasters seem to start occurring regularly and seem also to start looking much the same. Why not deal with the root cause? This question often leads to a rather circular discussion about the insufficiency of resources within the support group in question. To take it to an almost absurd extreme, all resources are too busy fighting fires in order to take time out for fixing any of the causes of the fires.

A manifestation of this situation that tends to be specific to IT revolves around the involvement of the Service Delivery function in the process of Solution Delivery. Most IT project management processes recognize the need to create capabilities and documentation specifically for successfully operating the IT assets to be delivered. Their quality and value depend upon an appropriate and timely investment by IT Operations in contributing to this work – at a minimum in reviewing the material produced on their behalf by other resources. Yet I have often observed, particularly during my consulting career while working on a large project, that this does not happen. Then the inevitable acrimonious discussion occurs (to the wry amusement of the clients) very late in the project and sometimes after a disaster happens (when amusement is in decidedly short supply) to the delivered solution:

"You didn't involve us," says Ops. "You didn't get involved when you were supposed to, and the project had a schedule to keep," says Projects. "Well we were all too busy dealing with your previous flawed implementations," rejoins Ops – somewhat passive-aggressively. It's definitely reminiscent of the "heroic" tendency in Service Delivery.

This is internecine warfare, which the CIO can't allow, or else s/he will suffer the direst consequences. And deservedly so. Deal with the challenge or die.

This leads logically to the second area of Service Delivery challenge, which is managerial. There has been some emphasis on managing Service Delivery "by the numbers" (and you'll be happy to hear that there will be considerably more, including these paragraphs). Establishing the "boss" metrics, and the diagnostics discussed in an earlier section of this chapter is just the beginning.

These performance metrics provide the means for effective management of software applications and their complex supporting IT infrastructure. The management in Service Delivery cannot simply be allowed to manage "by the seat of their pants," which Operations everywhere tends to prefer to do. The CIO must rise to the challenge of making his/her Service Delivery management use these numbers to control the quality of service delivered by software applications and for fact-based diagnosis and remedy of service issues.

Other than that, it's pretty much a piece of cake.

Lessons from the Trenches

Service Delivery summary

Service Delivery is a numbers game. That's another way of saying that it is best managed by letting the facts – as embodied in the measurements noted in this chapter – lead you.

There's no way to avoid the emotion and stress that is inherent in any operations role, so to be successful, Service Delivery managers have to have a high tolerance for stress, and have to develop techniques to deal with the emotion inherent in the role – especially when IT equipment and systems are failing and the clients are forced to struggle with "business as unusual." The best fundamental tool to do this (beyond the personal skills required to deal with the stress and the emotion) is measurement. It will tell you what is failing and why, and how to remedy the situation. And sharing this information with the client is what will ultimately make it possible to drain the emotion and stress from any given situation. So numerical and analytical skills are indispensable for success in Service Delivery. Choose your staff and your management accordingly.

Measurement in the Service Delivery context means the useful availability of application software (the "solutions" delivered to clients), and equivalent measures of the availability of all elements of the "technology stack" (all the things such as server and network, that have to be working in order for the application to be available to the client). The availability of elements of the technology stack provides "diagnostic" measures whereby Service Delivery staff can begin the diagnosis of what's going out of kilter. This is best done before some situation arises to cause the above-mentioned stress and emotional reactions.

All the rest, definitions of all the processes relevant to Service Delivery, and the best practices for managing them all, can be found in ITIL. So measure transparently, be sure to educate your Service Delivery teams in ITIL concepts, and success will be yours.

CHAPTER 5 ARCHITECTURE

The mission of the Architecture function is to plan for and to oversee the creation of an enterprise IT technical environment that is ever less expensive to make additions or changes to, and ever more flexible to accommodate them. One might safely add that Architecture should also ensure an ever more robust technical environment and a less risky one for adding new applications or updating old ones.

In order to effectively carry out this mission, Architecture has to establish and maintain a rigorously correct "blueprint" of the enterprise technical environment. Moreover, Architecture cannot be effective unless it has the power to disallow changes to the "as built" technical environment and the capability to create its own designs, and to effectively assess designs provided by others. This idea will be elaborated further, shortly.

Much like the Solution Delivery function, which is aided by the management knowledge and experience available in the Project Management Institute's Project Management Book of Knowledge, and like the Service Delivery function, which is similarly aided by the Information Technology Information Library, Architecture has its own certification bodies and bodies of knowledge. Unlike these other delivery functions that have a single dominant professional certification body, Architecture is blessed with multiple such bodies.

Certification and bodies of knowledge

The two dominant certification bodies are The Open Group Architecture Framework (TOGAF), and Zachman International. Both of these groups offer certification attesting to mastery by an individual practising Architect of a body of knowledge about the specific enterprise Architecture frameworks that these groups are promulgating. There are others, but they don't have as many adherents as these two.

In the Eastern Canadian context, it appears that most organizations that have regular interaction with the Canadian government (such as the Greater Toronto Airports Authority) have adopted TOGAF as their standard approach to Architecture. Organizations that have regular interaction with the Ontario public service (such as provincial government departments and their associated IT clusters, and various provincial crown corporations) have adopted the Zachman Framework.

My personal knowledge of these two frameworks and methodologies falls far short of that of a certified practitioner. However, from my perspective as an IT executive, although they appear to differ considerably, they are functionally equivalent in that they both provide a disciplined and practical framework for modelling an "as built" enterprise Architecture that is useful to the enterprise in various ways, including to the ongoing activities of Solution Delivery and Service Delivery. (Their modelling capabilities are not limited only to the "as built" scenario, but this is the one on which commentary will be focused in this book.)

A fully capable and mature Architecture Function proactively manages such a framework, whether based on the principles taught by TOGAF, by Zachman or by one of several other groups.

Support to other IT functions

An effective and engaged Architecture function, as owner of the "as built" technical blueprint, actively participates in the ongoing operations of the delivery groups, and takes on a crucial role in Strategic Alignment. What is involved in accomplishing this is outlined below.

To Solution Delivery

Architecture has a big role at several points in the PMI-defined project process groups. They amount to two major activities – although different gating processes at different enterprises might subdivide these into more than two.

Chronologically first is in support of the formulation of the business case. This provides a high-level technical approach and an estimate of the associated IT cost in the form of a market study or a similarly termed activity ("sample solution," or "solution assessment," as it was termed at the GTAA). There are various ways of doing this, which involve an informal survey of vendors in the marketplace (in conjunction with services provided by Forrester Research, Gartner or similar sources) and a formalized IT cost structure examining "one time" and "ongoing" IT costs, similar to the table set out earlier in the discussion about business case. Sometimes Architecture performs an overt survey (such as a "request for information," or RFI) of a selection of vendor products identified as being in the appropriate Gartner or Forrester quadrant.

Chronologically second is to act as the "design authority" by overseeing an overall design for a particular Solution. In that capacity, the Architecture group also must examine and approve the designs of components of the overall solution, as provided by outside vendors and internal teams, and how well they accommodate the overall concept, before the design gate can be successfully passed. Once the overall design has been rendered in such a way that it meets with the approval of Architecture management, the Solution Delivery project proceeds. This would be an appropriate point for Architecture to also update its TOGAF/Zachman "as built" model of the enterprise's technical environment, anticipating that the approved design will be delivered at "go live."

To Service Delivery

Architecture has an ongoing role in various ITIL-defined Service Delivery processes. For brevity's sake, I will summarize these to two.

First, in the problem management process, and some similar ones (such as incident management and event management), technical troubleshooting is required to identify the root cause of a problem. Once that is isolated, solution options must be evaluated and the appropriate one selected. Both in the troubleshooting activity, and in the choice of a solution (given that it is a design-like activity) Architecture have to involve themselves. They will not be the only source of expertise to the troubleshooting function, but they are unique in that they have the authority to withhold permission to proceed, if warranted. (They also have the obligation to clearly explain the reasons for withholding permission to proceed, so that the team wishing to do so knows what they have to change in order to gain their permission.)

Second, in the change management process, for similar reasons to the above, Architecture must be involved in the Change Advisory Board (CAB), the body that reviews and approves (or rejects, or postpones) ongoing changes to elements of the "as built" (e.g. security patches, proposed application additions and all the other myriad flow of more-or-less routine changes that must regularly be made as part of the ongoing business of running any substantial IT technical environment). As is the case for troubleshooting, Architecture is not the only group involved with the CAB. Unlike troubleshooting activities, Architecture is not the only group that has the authority to stop a particular change from proceeding as requested.

To Strategic Alignment

The availability of a comprehensive IT technical environment "blueprint," and an Architecture team knowledgeable in the software applications, networks and other elements of the technical environment, are both invaluable assets to whoever within IT is responsible for Strategic Alignment. As is the case with Strategic Alignment itself, there is no "one size fits all" methodology for applying this knowledge to an effective Strategic Alignment exercise, so it's more difficult to generalize about how this support is provided, than in the cases of Solution Delivery and Service Delivery.

The best I can do at this time is to give examples of some ways this Architecture support has been provided at different times and in different places.

Avoidance of "boys with toys" syndrome

Before getting into a few positive examples of how the Architecture function did its job at times and places in my experience, I want to tell you how it shouldn't be done.

The key departure from useful practice that I have seen in the past is the rather weak (sometimes entirely absent) consideration for the strategic direction of the enterprise that Architecture exhibits when reviewing new technologies. That is, the role of Architecture is diminished to simply ruling on what technologies, products and techniques are permitted, and those that are not, without consideration of specific elements of future plans. Whatever criteria are applied to determine what's "in" or "out," however wise and comprehensive, they have little value outside the context of the enterprise's strategy and of the IT function's strategic and operating plan. Yet I have worked at places (not as CIO) where this is the case.

Without explicitly considering that context, and the role of Architecture in making the overall enterprise investment ever more flexible and ever less expensive, architects are basically just playing with the newest technologies – "boys with toys."

Another way of labelling the interpretation of Architecture that I am describing here is the "technology police." That is, Architecture is reduced to maintaining a list of technologies and vendors that are "approved" for use in the enterprise employing them. In fact, most Architecture functions maintain such a list for various good reasons, so its existence isn't the problem. The problem is that there's often no economic, nor technical, and very little strategic context in support of the list.

In other words, I have observed that a particular technical product gets approved or disallowed by Architecture in isolation of any business case or project driving the request (let alone any enterprise-aligned technical strategy). So anyone gaining such approval has carte blanche to use the technology in any context that may seem appropriate after the approval.

This puts the cart before the horse, and reduces the very important Architecture function to a number of technical individuals "playing" with technologies and services that may or may not have relevance to the enterprise at some future time.

Clearly this situation is Mordac-like, almost a parody of what I have been writing about up until now. And yes, cross my heart, I have seen this waste of technical resources and the annoyance of everyone else with a bureaucratic process empty of any serious business purpose.

Examples of Architecture in IT organizations

These are all drawn from my personal experience, from organizations that I worked for as an employee for a period of several years. All are quite different in the way they viewed and utilized IT Architecture, but all in their own way achieved the Architecture mission – "ever less expensive and more flexible."

Lessons from the Trenches

Meeting the Architecture mission at de Havilland

First of all, I would like to invoke truth in advertising: at de Havilland there was no formal Architecture organization in my time as CIO (nor at any other time, as far as I know). Despite that, the de Havilland IT function succeeded over a period of several years to greatly reduce the cost of implementing new technologies and to greatly reduce the cycle time (increase flexibility) to implement new technology. Thus without a formal Architecture organization, it met the Architecture mission anyway.

This was a result of several happy accidents, including a laser-like focus on customer service. (Not that customer service or focus on it was an accident, but that the conscious focus on customer service led to serendipitous results that otherwise would have required the conscious efforts of an Architecture department.)

The contributing factors were an IT organization consisting of fully empowered Relationship Managers (i.e. managers totally in charge of all resources required to support each of engineering, manufacturing, finance, etc. as their particular clients) and a parent corporation intent on rationalizing all back-office and production functions to reduce the cost and the cycle time of producing airplanes.

When the IT organizational structure was revised along customer lines, it was intended to "empower" each of the Relationship Managers (they weren't called that, but it's clearly what their role was). It was very simple to allocate technical resources to all the managers responsible for a customer VP area. This was because each such area had distinct applications on the mainframe, servers and workstations that were specific to each VP area. That is, engineering design applications ran on IBM Unix workstations; manufacturing management applications ran on HP Unix workstations; customer support applications (and aircraft maintenance manuals produced by them) were implemented on Sun Microsystems Unix workstations; and all other business functions had their distinct applications on the mainframe. Programmers and server support specialists had already been assigned responsibility for specific applications, so having them report to new managers accountable to the business owners of these applications was straightforward. For that very reason, all internal knowledge of the technology involved was focused within each of the new departments. So in effect, the Relationship Managers "owned" the architectural expertise (and the project expertise, just incidentally) required for their "share" of the information systems and infrastructure. Knowledge of the network, and expertise in its management was held within the centralized operations department responsible for the technical health of the mainframe and of the campus shared network.

Shortly after the IT reorganization, the corporate initiative for reduced aircraft development cycle times drove us to modify the technical Architecture in two ways.

First, in support of Bombardier's desire to accommodate large but temporary engineering design teams at de Havilland, the senior technical folks in charge of the network (Architects by any other name) revised the campus network to be much faster and more resilient than it had been before. They also established a standardized wiring closet and a standardized network connection for any engineering (design or manufacturing) office. As a consequence, as engineering teams waxed and waned, IT had no further need to be involved in that process. The facilities department physically moved people in and out of office space, or built new space according to the "cookie cutter" IT wiring and connection standards. As a result the time and cost (and risk) to accommodate such team changes shrank to a small fraction of what it had been previously.

Second, in support of Bombardier's move to emulate Boeing's early success at "design/build" teams with its 777 aircraft (i.e. simultaneously designing a new plane to embody features and functions desired by the market, and to make it easily manufacturable), design engineering and manufacturing engineering applications that had previously supported a serial process (i.e. design first, and then figure out how to manufacture) were modified and/or replaced in some cases to accommodate the new parallel process. All the technical support to "re-architect" the new solution was available in house, although a lot of external talent had to be recruited to help with the end-user training in Catia – the software chosen to support the simultaneous design/build process. Again, the technical staff – internal and external – that provided Architecture support were not actually called Architects. The first new aircraft program that Bombardier applied the parallel design/build process to – the Global Express – reduced the time to market to about three years versus the previous five, with a corresponding reduction in the cost of the engineering teams required for that period of time.

So at de Havilland, in these ways we achieved – somewhat serendipitously – the Architecture mission without an Architecture department.

Architecture at The Globe and Mail

When the funding had been secured to finance a restructuring of the IT department at The Globe and Mail, the VP of HR, Mike Brophy, offered two pieces of advice. He suggested we hire a professional organizational design firm and that we hire highly qualified individuals for the new roles. In other words, he advised we lean strongly to over-hiring rather than under-hiring. I took his advice in both instances.

The organizational design consultant recommended a structure with three Directors reporting into the VP of IT: an Operations Director, whose team would focus on tasks one to three months out; a Projects Director, whose team would focus on tasks three to 12 months out; and an Architecture Director, whose team would focus on tasks 12 months to three years out (our strategic plan's horizon).

And so it was that we filled three new Director-level positions, including the brand-new function (for The Globe) of Director, Architecture.

The internal Globe IT black humour of the day observed that while we had an Architecture department, we had no Architecture to speak of – just a form of "Agriculture." That is, there probably were historical reasons for the evolution and growth of our seven distinct types of networks, multiple different types of personal computers and of servers that we owned, but there was no evident logic or design to it. They just grew – "evolved" would impute too much purpose and design behind the process. Among other things, we joked that if The Globe didn't have a particular brand or type of Unix server, then it didn't exist. It was "black" humour, because as a relatively small company (about 700 employees at the time), The Globe couldn't tolerate this much complexity, potential cost of change and inflexibility at any time – let alone when the enterprise was expecting to experience fierce competition with the need to adapt to it very quickly, very soon.

There was a lot of pressure on IT, and in particular on the Architecture team to get things done fast. We gave ourselves the first two years in the first three-year capital planning horizon to get the most important projects done. Constant and increasing pressure came from our IT counterparts at the Thomson Newspapers headquarters in Stamford, Connecticut, to exceed our plans, and to add scope to what plans there were. This led to many "fraternal" discussions between us and our IT brethren at corporate about how much "help" they were providing – but I digress.

Given the division of responsibility by "time span," Architecture had to develop and manage the three-year IT capital plan, which had an annual review. Projects executed the initiatives approved for the first year of the plan and all the carryover work from the previous budget year, but Architecture planned what was to be done when, and did a lot of the consensus building with the key user areas to confirm annual commitments. So Architecture in effect had to also become our Relationship Managers.

The task of building an internal consensus was a tough one for the Director of Architecture (I'll call him "Ken"), because his instructions from me were to also imbed the cost of rationalizing our infrastructure into the cost of each project business case. This was done in the interests of time, and of focus. It was clear that the existing IT infrastructure was a serious impediment to the newspaper's agility, both current and future. So sooner or later this rationalization would have to be done anyway. Moreover, much of the new technology we had to implement to help make the business more agile and flexible would be depending on a more rational IT infrastructure.

Most of our clients (or at least the contacts we worked with to create the IT capital plan) were fairly sophisticated in the economics and capabilities of IT. So of course, they recognized the extra costs and squawked bitterly at having to justify cleaning up this "technical mess on behalf of IT." Somehow, by dint of strenuous persuasion by Ken and his team (with occasional intervention by the CIO when it seemed likely that blood would flow), the principle was sold and we proceeded at a rapid pace to implement many modern newspaper systems, and to renew the underlying hardware and networks to support it.

By the time Conrad Black launched the National Post in competition with us for a lucrative advertising market – almost exactly two years into the new IT strategy – The Globe and Mail was ready. Seven distinct networks had been replaced by one more modern than any of its predecessors. The dozens of distinct types of PC models had been reduced essentially to two – one standard Wintel configuration, and one standard Mac configuration – each capable of running any of the newspaper's business applications.

Most front-line newspaper systems had been successfully replaced, and they operated on fewer numbers and brands of much more capable Unix servers.

In short, the business needs of The Globe and Mail had been met in time. It had new, modern and much more capable and reliable systems than it had ever had before. These systems had more capabilities to enhance and modernize the published product more quickly and flexibly than had ever before been the case.

Underlying all this was an IT infrastructure with a much lowered total cost of ownership that took fewer people to support, and which could be changed to meet any future business needs at much shorter notice than had earlier been possible.

The Architecture mission was met due to conscious organizational redesign, and due to the strenuous efforts of the new architecture team. (And especially of the hard-working and long-suffering Director – Ken. He never missed an opportunity to complain about the stress I "endowed" him with, but always did so with a smile.)

Architecture summary

As experience at de Havilland showed, it is possible to fulfill the Architecture role without a centralized and purposeful Architecture team. But that happy outcome requires the coincidence of a number of other factors, which is unlikely to happen very often. Therefore it is better for the CIO's eventual success and peace of mind to organize a "design authority" to which s/he delegates the responsibility to achieve the goal of making IT cheaper and more flexible in the long run.

The necessary ingredients for success are few. One, a method to model the enterprise's IT Architecture (e.g. TOGAF), and a software tool that allows the Architecture team to capture and maintain the salient facts about business process, software applications, data, infrastructure and the relationships between them all. Two, the authority from the CIO to force new investment and maintenance activities to conform to the Architecture plan. Three, a handful of intelligent and knowledgeable individuals, capable of formulating the plan and keeping it on track by involving themselves in the ongoing business of Strategic Alignment, Solution Delivery and Service Delivery.

Simple, right?

Well, actually no it's not. Having such an organization in being would obviously imply a very capable and mature IT function. It doesn't happen by fiat of the CIO (although if it did, that would be very nice, speaking personally).

For one thing, the Architecture talent and deep local knowledge necessary to achieve the mission does not grow on trees. It must largely be grown internally.

For another thing, how can one measure "how cheap," and "how flexible"? If one could, what are the benchmarks – what are good, better and best standards for each? If such measures exist, I am unaware of them – so if one of my readers is, then please get in touch with me. If they don't, then how do we as an IT management community develop them?

So, in conclusion it's my feeling that Architecture is an important function critical to IT's success. It is not yet as professional as it could be, due to the absence of objective measures of its progress in achieving its mission. So a CIO intent on his/her success must establish a strong Architecture function, and work with the community – internal and external – to develop and establish such measures.

CHAPTER 6 STRATEGIC ALIGNMENT

IT is a service function within most enterprises. As such it is useful and effective only to the extent that it directly contributes to the achievement of the overall enterprise's goals and objectives. So it is incumbent upon the IT function to clearly understand what these are, to both develop and to articulate a clear roadmap of IT's role in advancing them and to secure formal and transparent agreement from the enterprise that the proposed roadmap is the correct one.

The Strategic Alignment process amounts to IT finding out and confirming what are "the right things to do" as needed by the enterprise. Thus IT must know what new or improved IT assets (such as software application systems), and what new or improved IT services have to be delivered to make possible the outcomes that the enterprise aspires to in its strategic and operational goals.

What does all that mean, practically speaking? What does this IT roadmap look like?

It has to be related to the enterprise strategic plan. So let's step back briefly and consider what that would look like. In my experience the best and most useful enterprise strategic plans start out with quantifying what will be achieved over the multi-year planning horizon. For good governance, and for the clearest possible direction, objective measures of success must be in place. Nothing can be more black and white than quantitative measures and SMART goals. So goals and objectives are best expressed as improvements in such tangibles as sales, profits, operational efficiency, customer service, new (and existing) market penetration and others. This is "what" the enterprise intends to achieve. "How" this will be achieved over the time of the multi-year plan is also outlined in the form of specific actions and initiatives, such as improvements in business processes, and the creation of new capabilities. Usually in the strategic plan, the CEO also explicitly delegates responsibility for successfully carrying out groupings of these actions and initiatives to his or her direct reports – thus identifying the "who."

So to return to the IT roadmap: the basis of Strategic Alignment by IT to the enterprise strategy is the definition (what, how, who and when) of a multi-year project portfolio in which the completion of each project will contribute in a specific way to the successful achievement of these strategic actions and initiatives. An equally important element of the IT roadmap is the specification of resources and responsibilities for maintaining existing investment in IT assets – those that were delivered by past project portfolios, currently are an important underpinning to the current operations of the enterprise, and which, for the health of the enterprise, must be kept at the committed performance standards. The final element identifies the internal initiatives that IT will undertake to add new capabilities that will be needed by IT in the future, and to improve the effectiveness and efficiency of existing IT capabilities.

These three elements of the IT roadmap are usually provided in an annual IT strategic and operating plan. As part of the enterprise's annual budget process this strategic and operating plan puts forth the first year of a multi-year IT plan as the IT budget, but explicitly formatted to show clearly and concisely how it will align to the enterprise's strategic plan. It also summarizes all three elements of the IT roadmap and spending for the remaining years of the planning horizon. At its core it amounts to an approved IT project portfolio and a list of internal IT improvement initiatives, organized by year to be completed within the enterprise planning horizon. This may be three years, five years, or even only the budget year if the enterprise has no formal multi-year planning process.

The clear expectation, and the best practice that I have found in my experience, is that this IT roadmap will be reviewed and updated annually – in effect it becomes a rolling multi-year plan, just as the most effective enterprise strategic plans are.

Lessons from the Trenches

Approval by the enterprise of the IT strategic and operating plan is the equivalent to agreement that if IT carries out what's in that plan, then it's "aligned." It is in the interests of the CIO and his/her direct reports to communicate the contents of that plan both internally to their IT teams and externally to their customer community. It should be well understood both by the IT delivery teams and by their team's clients, and it should be used as the foundation for expectation management during the coming budget period.

How is it achieved?

In my experience the best approach is completely straightforward – just go out and ask your colleagues in the business what they need from IT. Have a series of conversations about it. Use the occasion of whatever planning process the enterprise utilizes. Get on the clients' agenda during appropriate dates on the planning calendar, and tell them: "We in IT want to be doing the right things, and we need to know what you think they are."

Prepare for these conversations. Everyone should make themselves familiar with the existing IT roadmap, and with the enterprise strategy. These are inputs to the annual conversation IT will have with its clients to update IT's alignment to the business. The outputs of these discussions will be proposals for updates to the remaining annual plans in the remainder of the planning horizon (e.g. in a five year planning scenario, Years 2 to 5 of the old plan roll over to Years 1 to 4 of the new plan, and a brand new Year 5 is formulated).

You may find it quite surprising how short and to the point such discussions usually are. In a focused, strategically minded organization, IT gets it marching orders quickly and clearly. In less-focused, less strategically oriented, less objective measurement-focused enterprises, it is much more difficult for IT to determine "the right things to do."

Challenges with the IT strategic and operating plan

IT project portfolio – project priorities

IT's most visible contribution to the enterprise strategic plan is through the IT project portfolio. Each project delivers (or is intended to deliver) features, functions and capabilities provided in software applications that enable the enterprise to do its business "faster, better, cheaper." So the project portfolio is made up essentially of projects that implement new software applications with brand new features and functions, upgrade existing ones to augment existing features and functions, or improve the service levels (e.g. performance, availability, recoverability) of existing systems. They are all projects that have to "make it to the list" to define "the right things to do" for IT.

Arriving at a consensus as to what this list should consist of is a more demanding and less straightforward exercise than it may seem. This is primarily due to the indirect nature of IT investment. However the enterprise expresses its strategic goals (e.g. in terms of year-over-year improvement in a key metric), any investment in IT can only provide the enterprise with certain capabilities. These capabilities have no value in and of themselves. Their value is realized when the enterprise successfully uses them (usually as only one of many means) to achieve the improved metrics that have been defined as the goals of the enterprise strategic plan.

This indirect nature of IT investment outcomes introduces significant opportunities for ambiguity when the enterprise wishes to determine IT project priorities.

In the first place, this means that calculating the return on investment for information technology is quite problematic when most of the time, no direct benefit can be ascribed it – only a cost – and attempts to do so often strain credulity. Lacking the means to calculate an ROI, one is robbed of the best tool available to rank an investment.

To be clear: I would expect that a corporate initiative intended to achieve a significant element of the enterprise strategic plan will have a strong business case. However, the IT investment is usually only one of the inputs to the business case. There are many others, such as extra staff, a change in the organizational structure, change of bricks and mortar facilities or investment in other hard assets. The sum of costs of all these inputs is the cost of the business case. The benefits achieved through the combination and application of all these inputs provide an ROI. It is not practical or useful to calculate an ROI ascribable to only one of the inputs – such as the IT investment.

In the second place, when it comes to investment in IT, there are always more opportunities (and "pet projects," frankly) than there is free cash flow to finance them, or IT capacity to deliver them. In the absence of an ROI, passion, eloquence, strength of personality and political influence become the tools of choice for purposes of ranking investments.

Finally, often a very large and confusing goals and objectives cascade is created when the corporate goals and objectives (the enterprise strategic plan, as owned by the CEO) are subdivided and delegated down the corporate hierarchy. This cascade consists of initiatives for various corporate executives to complete in order to be successful (and of course for the enterprise to be successful as an outcome of that). Given the sheer number of these goals and objectives, even in relatively small enterprises, it is easy to lose sight of how many of these initiatives are related, that they are often subsets of each other. Sometimes in poorly managed strategic planning processes some of them actually work to negate each other – or so it seems to the poor lambs (of whom I was often one) trying to create a consensus as to what projects should be in the IT project portfolio – and which ones shouldn't be.

IT assets in place – results of past priority projects

An unfortunately less visible contribution to the enterprise strategic plan is the portfolio of assets already in place. These are application systems and all the associated IT infrastructure (servers, networks, workstations and other elements of information technology) delivered by previous IT projects, which were required and assumed to operate over a considerable lifespan at some nominal standard of performance in order to continue delivering the capabilities required by previous enterprise strategic plans.

Given that the typical life of an IT application system, for depreciation purposes, is around five years, the enterprise's investment in IT capabilities that are already in place is about five times the cost of the current planning year's investment in IT projects. In this day and age, the enterprise is dependent upon the continued "dial tone" reliable operation of its IT assets in place. This dependency is often critical in that if one or more "key" systems is down, the enterprise simply cannot do business until service is restored. One would naturally assume therefore that some serious thought would be given to investing in the ongoing health of these assets.

The challenge is: how does one decide which ones to invest in, and in what way? In my mind, this is a blatant example of "you don't manage what you don't measure."

If the IT Service Delivery function has performance measures of the kind discussed in the section on Service Delivery, then what to invest in and how, isn't a very big challenge. But what if such measures are not in place? How will the CIO (or anyone else for that matter) know what to invest in? What systems? For what reasons? Invest in the application, the infrastructure, the people or the process? What kind of a conversation will the CIO be able to have with his/her colleagues when arriving more or less naked of quantitative logic, or indeed of the particulars of what needs to be improved, to advocate for such investments?

Or, if the CIO avoids these sorts of conversations due to lack of information and fear of embarrassment, how about the conversation that ensues in the absence of such regular monitoring and investment? You know – when a key system "craters"? For more insight on this, review the section on Service Delivery.

In any case, I leave it to your imagination. Trust me, if you haven't personally gone through the pain and suffering, humiliation and regret involved in the latter conversation like I have, there is no way on Earth your imagination will come close to the reality.

The challenge of enterprise capability and maturity

Prior to completing this book, I posted excerpts from the evolving work on LinkedIn. Among the many useful and thought-provoking comments, I received back a couple from a seasoned IT professional. First, he observed that IT really couldn't outperform the "state of the art" at its host enterprise. I will briefly (and narrowly) speak to this point in the rest of this section. The second point was that along with the model of IT governance, and the set of rules of how to work within it, it may be useful to formulate and articulate a capability and maturity model of IT. I agree that it would be useful to do so, but I didn't set out to include such an idea in this book. Moreover, I don't have much experience in managing within such a concept. Consequently this book will not address it directly. However, the more I thought about this matter, the more relevant it seemed to me as a subject of future exploration – a launch point for the next stage in the development of IT management, perhaps. Stay tuned. I issue a challenge to you, dear reader, to do something about this idea, later in the book.

It may not be obvious from the discussion above, or from the comments of this one book reviewer, but to be successful at Strategic Alignment, an IT organization needs to be working for a relatively sophisticated enterprise. The enterprise has to have a clear, broadly understood and above all, a quantified vision of its own future, among many other management capabilities. So the capability and maturity of the IT function – and its ability to deliver superior results – depend very much on the management capability and maturity of the enterprise of which it is a part.

A real problem that many CIOs face is that what the IT strategy ought to be is often not so easy to figure out. Many organizations unfortunately do not have a formal strategic plan, or if they have a document that purports to serve this purpose oftentimes it does not specify any particular outcomes or activities, nor does it assign accountability for successful action. My observation is that the state of the art in strategic and operational planning is still rather poor. Outside of a relatively very few large businesses, the strategic plan of most enterprises is no more than a somewhat poetic "feel good" statement evoking a future to which the organization aspires, without much of a clue provided as to how this will be achieved, what it will look like once it is achieved or what will be measured to define "achievement." In the absence of actionable criteria, and some quantitative method of tracking progress, what IT can do and how this might be helpful let alone what are the right things for IT to do can only be pretty much guesswork.

The danger to the enterprise is that this will drive the IT function to focus on delivering "shiny new toys" that particularly strong personalities within the business can be successful at championing. These may or may not enable the business to deliver on its goals and strategy, but they will certainly consume IT management bandwidth and the enterprise's cash and human resources. It will also tend to lead the enterprise to ignore IT assets that are already in place, and upon which the enterprise may depend for success. To ignore them, that is, until these critical systems fail, in which case IT is excoriated without regard to the failing IT assets operational criticality or any other logic. If that sounds bitter, my apologies. As explanation, I simply offer up that some wounds aren't given a reasonable period to heal.

It is the responsibility of the CIO and her/his leadership team to work at overcoming this problem – to delve to the heart of the mystery. However they succeed in doing so (and there are many ways to skin this particular cat, some of which are discussed below), they will be doing the organization a great service by helping it identify and prioritize the best investments in IT. They will also be taking another big step toward the justification of their own survival and prosperity.

How to put the IT roadmap together?

My preferred form of the IT roadmap, and the one I have most frequently seen in my travels in the trenches, is the IT strategic and operating plan. This is a multi-year plan that amounts to a detailed annual budget for the first year of the planning horizon, and summarized versions of this for all subsequent years. It has two chief advantages: first, it is an efficient way to extend thinking of the future beyond just the coming year, since in almost all enterprises, a budget has to be prepared anyway; second, it provides for an annual refresh of the strategic plan, based on the previous year's performance, lessons learned and some new thinking that likely happened after last year's plan was finalized.

It should be noted that the actual budget preparation in most cases comes fairly late in the annual planning cycle. Preparation of the strategic and operating plan should start much earlier than that – as early in the planning process as possible.

IT project portfolio

Determining the IT project portfolio should be the first order of business. This must be done in consultation with the executives of the enterprise, and their direct reports, when these individuals start considering – with the CEO – what their goals and objectives will be for the coming and subsequent years. In the event a clear and viable multi-year plan is already in place, with well thought-out initiatives to achieve it, IT's job is relatively simple: take part in the discussions to update the old multi-year plan and determine what changes will require IT investment, how and when.

As the enterprise strategic plan and the initiatives to achieve it (the CEO's and other executives' goals and objectives) are firmed up, so should the IT project portfolio.

New capabilities for IT

This is the time to consider whether changes to IT's capabilities will be required. For example, if in the current year's planning discussions, the enterprise decides on an initiative to make its first foray into eCommerce for good commercial reasons, then not only does an "eCommerce project" or two have to be inserted into the IT project portfolio, but IT has to figure out how to put the skills and capabilities in place to deliver this solution. If IT has never done anything of the kind before and the capability doesn't yet exist, then it has to be somehow acquired. It can be developed internally utilizing the skills and knowledge of both new and existing employees, or an external provider can be found who has the skills already, or some combination. The initiative to develop an eCommerce capability within IT must be defined, and it must win its place in the IT strategic and operating plan by "demonstrating" how the chosen approach will best advance the enterprise's strategic plan.

Performance of existing IT assets

This is also the time to look at the performance of IT assets in place. There are two cases to consider: first, if the IT function of the enterprise does not have performance measurement of IT assets in place, along the lines set out in the section on Service Delivery, then the most strategic initiative that the CIO can possibly advocate for, is to actually put it into place; and second, one can actually then consider to look at the performance of IT assets in place, once there are measures to do so.

In the second case, in my experience most IT assets and the support teams perform well, delivering the performance and availability that the enterprise requires to deliver expected business results. One should expect that for a few assets – a minority of the installed base – that either an improvement to the currently targeted performance will provide a significant business opportunity, or the currently targeted performance levels are chronically not being met. In the latter instances, IT must find a way to meet the targeted performance levels, (since this an unmet IT obligation) and for each such asset include an initiative to carry it out in the IT strategic and operating plan. In the former case, IT must perform the analysis of available alternatives to build the best approach to exploit the opportunity into either the IT project portfolio, the IT operating budget, or in short wherever in the enterprise's economic planning it best fits.

It is important to note that any initiative to improve the performance of an existing asset is a problem-solving exercise. Only one of the available methods – and often not the appropriate one – is to add a project to the IT project portfolio with the idea of modifying the asset in some way. Often, investments in staff training, process, or in improved vendor performance are the way to go. This will be determined from the Service Delivery performance measures that are in place, and the insights provided by the client and the support team. In my experience this recognition comes about organically as a result of the ongoing engagement of the client in the almost continuous review and discussion of the ongoing performance of existing IT assets.

Review of past year's performance

An objective assessment of the previous year's performance should be performed. What projects, actions, and initiatives that were supposed to be completed, in fact were not? Should they be carried forward into the new plan? If so, how? What assumptions were made that turned out to be true? Which ones weren't?

This review will clearly have an important impact on the IT project portfolio, but missing planning targets (or even exceeding them) in other areas can be significant also.

IT SWOT analysis

An honest and forthright SWOT (Strengths, Weaknesses, Opportunities, Threats) analysis of IT should be performed by the CIO and his/her management team. To the extent appropriate to the enterprise strategy, actions and initiatives should be considered to take advantage of Strengths and Opportunities, while mitigating Weaknesses and Threats. Much of this will reflect the previously mentioned work, but some of it will not, so I highly recommend that the CIO and IT management hold such an exercise every year. More about SWOT analysis a little bit later in this section.

Iterations of the strategic and operating plan

All this "strategic material" – draft IT project portfolio, changes to IT capabilities driven by the enterprise strategy, needed improvements to the performance of IT assets in place, review of the past year's performance, and the outcomes of the SWOT analysis – is brought together into a draft IT strategic and operating plan. The first iteration can be quite "drafty," but it should cover all the ground – at least a first pass consulting all clients, and developing all the strategic material. For best results, there should be a few iterations, played back to the clients and if possible also to cross-client groups, soliciting their feedback. This is a valuable technique both in that it assists transparency and in that it abets constructive criticism of the evolving IT roadmap.

As a rule of thumb, two iterations would be good, and three would be better, but probably no more, so as to minimize the risk of boring your colleagues and clients with the subject and your faces. For best results, the timing of the iterations should be congruent with the enterprise planning calendar and timelines. That is, each review session should be close to the time that the enterprise strategic plan is augmented or fleshed out in some way so that the clients of IT are fresh from updating their own thinking about the future and therefore are likely to have some new thoughts about how to better utilize IT in their operations as the future unfolds.

The guiding principle here is to accept that "planning is a public process, not a private event." (No, I don't know where the quote comes from, but it makes so much sense that I'd be happy to claim it myself if no attribution can be found.) This is certainly true for a service organization like IT, if not for everyone.

With each iteration, there will be fewer open items to be resolved, and more clarity about the IT roadmap – about what are "the right things to do" for IT. As a final result there will be a completed and approved IT strategic and operating plan that is fairly well understood and bought-into by the senior management of the enterprise.

Chapter 6 Strategic Alignment

How is Strategic Alignment measured?

Much as for the Architecture function, it seems straightforward in principle what one should measure about the effectiveness of Strategic Alignment. There are two major classes of measurement.

First, how well does IT turn out to be aligned with the enterprise, year over year. In other words, in objectives terms, how well focused is IT on enterprise priorities?

Second, how well does IT deliver on "the right things to do," which amounts to an annual report card on all of the department.

For me the first area is the challenge. I am unaware of any quantitative measures in practical use that assess the success of the Strategic Alignment function. And in keeping with earlier discussions, this measure is not entirely in IT's control. The propensity of the enterprise to "change its mind" within the planning cycle (as opposed to "update" its thinking at the annual review) makes any attempt by IT to align itself to the business akin to shooting at a moving target. Strategic Alignment under these circumstances is not impossible, but the risk is that the IT roadmap would have to be updated so often as to be a bit of a joke.

One clear indicator of this enterprise changeability is the rate of change of the IT project portfolio over the course of the planning year. I have been with organizations where the projects authorized and underway at the end of the year have been changed by 50% to 60% from the project portfolio authorized and funded at the beginning of the year. Usually, this has meant a simple accretion to the original portfolio without any "de-escalation" of projects within earlier versions of the portfolio. Apart from the practical problems this presents to IT management regarding the requirement to form new teams and to staff and resource them well within any reasonable time fence, one has to seriously question the enterprise's understanding of strategy. If within less than one fiscal year, the enterprise's view of what IT investments are required to support its long-term strategy changes so much, then how much credibility does the strategy deserve?

On the other hand, how well did the IT Strategic Alignment function capture the ideal IT project portfolio during the planning process itself? A poorly managed and executed alignment process could also account for the kind of situation described above, so that IT finds itself largely confused over which projects are important and which are not so much. So we feel compelled to "do everything," and so scramble at the last minute for Project Managers and other resources to make it all happen.

The above two paragraphs outline qualitatively what poor Strategic Alignment looks like. A quantitative measure or two would be more useful, although as mentioned earlier, I am unaware of any. Until such a measure is developed, lack of it stands in the way of any IT capability and maturity model.

The need to formulate such measures and to put them to general use is a pretty important priority for any CIO. Until such measures are in place for the purpose of guiding management of the process, Strategic Alignment is an existential challenge for IT, and makes it very difficult for IT to "shine" in all the delivery performance measurements that are available. It also makes it difficult for the enterprise to assess objectively how well the IT function is managed, and while the executive management of the enterprise may be content to remain unaware of this issue, it would be a career-prolonging move for the CIO to raise this issue, and solve it.

Why is this so? Because in its absence, the CIO ("Career is Over," remember?) depends in this area at least on political skill and popularity to survive. It would be better for the CIO's reputation and compensation to depend more on actual delivery – objectively measured

Chapter 6 Strategic Alignment

Approaches to Strategic Alignment

In the following few pages, I will set out a few approaches I have observed in my own experience, and then will provide what I hope will be a useful generalization.

Ideal situation (Bombardier, Thomson Corp.)

The ideal situation for a conscientious CIO "alignment-wise," is where the greater organization formally manages both an explicit strategy and a detailed strategic and operating plan, and also holds corporate management responsible for goals and objectives directly related to this strategic and operating plan. This is the best possible ecosystem for IT to organize itself "to do the right things."

Terminology varies quite a bit from enterprise to enterprise, since strategic planning is not really a standardized practice. However, the concepts are not difficult, and in almost all cases where an organization adopts an actionable strategic plan it's pretty easy to figure out what terms apply to which concepts.

The organization's strategic goals or objectives, to be actionable, are expressed in SMART terms (Specific, Measurable, Agreed-Upon, Relevant and Time-bound). Strategic goals are by their nature very ambitious and very difficult to achieve. They each require one or more strategic initiatives (think of them as really big projects with a really broad scope) to deliver the desired results.

A strategic initiative will itself tend to be very large and very complex. It will almost certainly be transformational (i.e. will change business processes and/or business hierarchies) and will probably be cross-functional. It may require several years to fully complete. Successful completion will be defined by achievement of one or more SMART goals or objectives that relate strongly to the original strategic goal – likely being some closely related subset. Responsibility for successful completion is usually assigned to a senior executive. This Executive Sponsor will enlist the appropriate level of management from all the other business functions involved, and together they will subdivide the initiative into parts for which the sponsor will delegate responsibility, therefore including measures defining successful completion of subordinates' and colleagues' part of the work.

In this way, all strategic goals are divided up and delegated to the appropriate parts of the enterprise through a set of strategic initiatives driving a cascade of goals and objectives across all functions and all the levels of the management hierarchy, from the CEO (who owns the enterprise's strategic plan) down to the most junior level of management that participates in the formal goal- and objective-setting process.

As a fully participating member of the management team, the CIO will have her/his delegated subset of these goals and objectives. It will consist entirely of new investments in information technology assets – whether to provide new capabilities, to make the operation of existing assets more reliable or responsive, to provide more capacity in some area, or something similar to all the above. This set of IT initiatives and the ways it relates to the larger enterprise goals and objectives is the starting point for alignment, and it is the essential raw material for the IT strategic plan.

The CIO will in turn delegate these IT initiatives in a logical manner to her/his organization. They are the IT portfolio representing "what" IT must deliver to the business over the time horizon of the strategic plan. Changes to the "how" IT delivers them over the same time horizon determines the IT strategic plan. That is, if the various functions of IT reporting to the CIO must develop new capabilities, new skills, new knowledge, or new capacities in order to make the delivery possible, then these organizational transformations or outsourcings define the rest of the IT strategic plan.

To complete the IT strategic plan, the CIO and her/his management team should then back and perform a realistic and formal assessment of IT's capability to deliver on all these projects. A good way is to perform a SWOT analysis of IT through one or more facilitated workshops involving the IT leadership team (CIO and direct reports), other more junior IT management and possibly some senior professionals.

The intent of this exercise is to enlist all viewpoints in the exercise so as to improve the odds that the IT organization can actually deliver on all the projects defined in the IT portfolio and on the services (planned and current) in the IT service catalogue. It will find ways to remedy internal weaknesses and play to internal strengths. It will find ways to mitigate external threats and to take advantage of external opportunities. IT's strategic issues (subjects of concern to IT management, not fitting neatly into any of the SWOT categories) will be raised and the means to resolve them will be determined. Ownership of all the above will be assigned.

All this IT SWOT material is then combined with the IT portfolio to create a complete IT strategic plan that contains an immense amount of useful detail.

It is advisable that the CIO and her/his direct reports summarize this information into a useful communications document. The purpose of such a document is to play back what they understand to be the expectations of the IT function's customers (i.e. the rest of the enterprise) to its customer base and to solicit feedback as to whether the IT leadership actually "got it." This feedback should be incorporated and the agreement of the customer base that IT has now captured "the right things to do" should be recorded and publicized. The evidence of IT Strategic Alignment is now available for all to see.

The final product should be presented to various customer forums to more broadly confirm that IT has "got it." It should also be presented to all the management and staff of the IT function so that they understand customer expectations sufficiently to carry them out, but also to inspire them with concrete evidence of the value and impact of IT on the rest of the organization.

Lessons from the Trenches

For the record, the preceding model and process of IT Strategic Alignment describes the situation at Bombardier Aerospace while I was CIO at its de Havilland Division. Bombardier has an excellent strategic planning system – which quite openly and unashamedly steals from the process developed over many very successful decades by Emerson Electric. Bombardier (and Emerson) provide the "gold standard" for strategic planning. Any CIO fortunate enough to be employed by either of these organizations will have "alignment" handed to her/him on a plate.

Similarly the Thomson Corp. (while I was with The Globe and Mail, the newspaper was part of it), also had a well-developed large corporation strategic planning process. It was not as rigorous and detailed as the system at Bombardier, but very effective all the same. It was strongly focused on outcomes and the management reward systems – both short term and long term – were tightly integrated into actually achieving the various multi-year goals and objectives of the strategy. In that environment, it was relatively easy for me and my team to effect alignment and deliver what the enterprise needed. Most of my preoccupation turned out to be inward-looking – i.e. how did IT have to be tweaked to make it all happen the way it should.

Not all organizations are as disciplined as Bombardier and Thomson, which have a strategic plan supported by a cascade of goals and objectives methodically across all business functions and down to a fairly junior level of management, and then live and die by that planning. So how should IT management deal with the alignment issue in such circumstances?

Well, that depends on what planning sophistication is missing in the enterprise. I will provide a few examples from my own experience and will wrap up with some (I hope) useful generalizations.

The other extreme (Canada Wire and Cable)

In the early 1980s, I became the CIO of Canada Wire and Cable. At the time, CWC had about $1 billion annual turnover, making it by far the largest manufacturer of wire and cable in Canada. It had also acquired Carol Cable, one of the largest such companies in the U.S. CWC was only one of several large manufacturing enterprises owned by Noranda Mines. As such, they were part of Noranda's diversification into the downstream processing of the copper and other metals that the parent company mined worldwide.

CWC dominated the wire and cable business in Canada and was a big player in the U.S., but its market position was being nibbled at by foreign competition (primarily by Alcatel, a French-based conglomerate). The reasons for this were numerous, but two were high on the list. First, there was a strong and growing suspicion that CWC's cost structure was too high. Second, and the most obvious, was that CWC's administrative processes were very much paper-driven. They were cumbersome, inefficient and utterly inadequate as a source of management information about CWC's business.

Discontent ran deep within the customer-facing parts of the enterprise over how primitive the administrative systems at CWC were, and how negatively they intruded upon the customer experience. CWC's sales staff were utterly unable to support customer inquiries about availability of product, about open order status or about historical order volumes, as just three examples. All the competition provided more rapid, more efficient and more responsive customer service. The embarrassment and unhappiness over the company's backwardness had been transmitted to the executive management of CWC by various channels, including directly by many valued customers.

There was a growing pressure on enterprise management to "do something."

Attempts by all parties, including my predecessor, the conscientious head of IT, to take positive action by investing in computer systems, got very little traction. Skunkworks projects and trials using existing somewhat inadequate systems and infrastructure demonstrated very tangible success, but executive management was focused elsewhere.

Looking back, it's clear that however informal, alignment as to what "the right things to do" for IT truly existed between the IT leader of the day and his clients in sales, distribution and manufacturing management. The gap existed further up in the hierarchy.

CWC executive management was very interested in extending its reach into the development and manufacture of fibre-optic cable. The capital investment for this program was substantial, requiring approval from executives at Noranda corporate offices. At that level, a polite but rather pointedly unfavourable comparison was made between that desire to go "high tech" and their "green eyeshades and quill pens" method of managing their customer relations, their supply chain and manufacturing operations.

So by withholding approval of CWC executive management's initiative into fibre optics, the shareholders at Noranda Inc. demonstrated that they were aligned with middle management's desire for a strategy to "put the house in order" (including where appropriate, investments in IT). Sometime during that internal debate over the direction of the enterprise, I was hired as CIO and given the mandate to "catalyze" a useful solution.

CWC was already one of the heaviest computer users of the Noranda Group. They were the single largest customer of the in-house service bureau – Norcomp. A few of the Toronto-area CWC plants were using some of Norcomp's software for customer order processing, and there was a pilot project to extend this application to the magnet wire plant in Simcoe, Ontario, about 150 kilometres southwest of Toronto. There was also an MRP (manufacturing requirements planning) pilot project using Norcomp facilities at CWC's Leaside manufacturing plant in Toronto.

Unfortunately none of this activity was helping point the way to a scalable solution set for CWC executives. The capabilities of the administrative systems and services available from Norcomp were minimal – appropriate for a far-flung mining and smelting operation, but insufficiently sophisticated for a manufacturing operation with a dozen plants and thousands of customers. Even if CWC management were interested in rolling out these simpler systems to all factories, warehouses and sales offices in North America, the very high costs to scale up seemed to overpower any realistic business case.

I worked hard with the Norcomp team, who were open and co-operative. But frustratingly for all of us, it eventually became obvious that Norcomp could not find a way to stretch or bend its basic mandate to provide inexpensive shared solutions to the Noranda mining and metal refining operations and at the same time economically provide a unique set of compute- and data-intensive manufacturing solutions to CWC.

So we had to look elsewhere.

CWC had a very successful and cost-effective distributor in Houston. It happened to be using a commercially available software package to manage customer orders and inventory. That package was adapted for use by CWC (becoming the National Order Processing System, or NOPS) and was successfully rolled out to 25 locations in North America within 12 months, rapidly and effectively removing the most painful "thorn in the paw" of CWC's sales and distribution management.

The Leaside plant's MRP system (an early precursor to what is now known as enterprise requirements planning, or ERP) was converted to operate on the same line of minicomputers that was utilized for the NOPS. This made it possible to scale the solution from that single plant to the remaining 11. Thus eventually the "thorn in the paw" of manufacturing management promised to also be removed. I had departed for a new job at Magna International before this happened.

These were IT Solution Delivery successes, but not Strategic Alignment successes. There was no practical way that IT could be aligned to the enterprise, since the enterprise was debating within itself about the right vision for the future. It continued to do so for a while. Just a few years later, Noranda merged with Falconbridge, which then sold off the wire and cable manufacturing operations to Alcatel. So CWC ceased to exist as an independent entity and IT Strategic Alignment became moot.

In any case, since the enterprise could not formulate a consistent and coherent strategy acceptable to all management, IT was stymied in any efforts it made to align. Hence, this example is at the other end of the spectrum of the "ideal" situation.

A pragmatic approach (Conductores Monterrey)

While I was with CWC, I was introduced to what looked at the time (and still does) like "the promised land" of pragmatic IT Strategic Alignment at a Mexican company called Conductores Monterrey.

This was an affiliate of CWC, in which the Canadian company had an equity interest. I was directed to visit their operations and to study particular aspects of their financial and IT functions.

CWC policy was to invest in wire and cable manufacturers in countries such as Mexico, Nigeria and Australia that were not as far along as Canada in building rural electrical power and telephone networks. The strategy was to let the wire and cable manufacturing enterprises in these countries benefit from Canadian know-how (and thus pay royalties and licence fees for technology to CWC) but to deliberately avoid the risk of managing these foreign companies by taking on a minority interest – typically 30% to 40% of the ownership. At that level of investment, CWC would enjoy the technical fees, participate in profits through dividends and exercise considerable influence through the Board of Directors over ongoing policy.

So as a matter of policy, CWC preferred these foreign operations to be majority-owned and managed by local nationals. In the case of Conductores Monterrey, this was the Garza family who, in addition to the wire and cable manufacturing company in Nuevo Laredo had many other investments across Mexico in other manufacturing and in other commercial activities as disparate as agriculture and Volkswagen dealerships.

The entire conglomerate's IT function was managed by an East Texan by the name of Jim Gebhart. He was under a long-term contract to the Garzas to create, manage and leave behind a smoothly functioning IT department when his contract was completed. At the time I made my visits, he had been there for some years, but his contract had recently been extended and updated to the mandate that has just been described.

Jim was an interesting guy. We talked about many things that I found illuminating, but the most striking aspect to me was that he had organized his monthly calendar to concentrate almost exclusively on alignment.

He had 10 direct reports, all but one of whom (the manager of the Burroughs mainframe operations) were responsible for the IT services to a set of Garza business operations (and only one of these was Conductores Monterrey). Each of these managers had a staff commensurate with the resources required to fulfill the needs of their client. Jim and each such manager had a monthly meeting with the executive management of each operation once per month. The agenda was in only two parts: how did we perform against last month's commitments, and do the next few months' commitments need to be updated for any reason?

Given the need to travel around Mexico to the customer sites, about half of Jim's month was consumed in the monthly meetings, and the other half was consumed in progress reviews and consultations in preparation for future monthly meetings. Jim's IT department seemed very effective, was certainly well regarded far beyond the confines of the Garza family's business interests, and I believe owed a very large part of this good reputation to the pains he and his team took to stay in alignment (and to consistently deliver according to the agreed "right things to do").

This is a simple and straightforward approach to Strategic Alignment. Clearly it was effective at Conductores Monterrey those many years ago. I adapted aspects of it to the situation at de Havilland quite a few years later, with some success.

So to any CIO entering into a new mandate, I highly recommend starting with the Conductores Monterrey approach and modifying it as time and circumstances require.

One last example – (Sherritt Gordon Mines)

My first CIO job was with Sherritt Gordon Mines, a company with mining operations in northern Manitoba and with a complex refining operation northwest of Edmonton at Fort Saskatchewan, Alberta. There was a fertilizer sales office based in Edmonton. The company's head office was in Toronto, from where they sold all other company products, principally metals and the products of their independent mint, and managed a number of overseas investments. Each geographic nexus of the company had its own independent IT department. There was a total absence of synergy between these independently operating IT departments.

I was not yet 30 years of age when I landed this job, and the truth is that Strategic Alignment was handed to me on a plate. The CFO and some other senior management at each of the operating divisions had decided that the IT function needed to be somehow merged into a critical mass with sufficient inter-divisional synergy so that it would be capable of taking on large projects as required for any part of the company. I was hired as head of IT (that was too long ago for the CIO designation to have any currency), and told to make it happen.

There was no change in the formal IT organization. All the IT operations that had been independent prior to my arrival remained independent and reporting to their own divisional management. I had influence thanks to a lot of executive support but no hierarchical power. The executive support came from the original group of executives who had decided what IT should do and why – and formally structured themselves into an IT Steering Committee after I came on board.

With the support and guidance of that group, I and my colleagues built a corporate data centre at Fort Saskatchewan, purchased a mainframe computer, established data communications links from all company locations to that data centre, converted all systems (from three different platforms) and trained all IT staff to use the new corporate platform. We incurred the new costs of building the data centre, of buying the computer, and of additional staff to manage the data centre – but substantially reduced total company-wide IT costs from what they had been before the consolidation.

We proved that the new organization was capable of taking on large new projects by soon afterwards building a sophisticated new proprietary geostatistical system for the mining division. This system was needed to analyze the complex copper-zinc ore body below the 2,000-foot level at the Ruttan Mine. The analytical method to calculate the ore reserves was a new approach – required because none of the conventional calculation methods (and available software tools) of the day could do the job.

A team of analysts and programmers from all three major company operations (Toronto, Fort Saskatchewan, northern Manitoba) collaborated with the mining geologists and their consultants from academe to create this system. It was developed "just in time." Design and programming was simultaneous with the deep drilling program that sampled the potential ore body. Programming and testing of the major graphics functions were completed just weeks before the final analysis of the Ruttan ore body was completed.

The exercise was an IT strategic triumph. We created a synergistic IT organization at less cost than the previous decidedly non-synergistic one. We proved its synergy by delivering a complex new solution under very tight timelines, using resources from widely separated parts of the enterprise.

Unfortunately the business was not so triumphant. The "answer" returned by the new system was that the ore body below 2,000 feet at Ruttan was "marginal." Shortly afterwards there was a sharp drop in metal prices, turning what appeared to be a marginally economic ore body into what was undoubtedly the equivalent of "rock" until the rebound of metal prices – some years in the indeterminate future. The good news is that as a consequence of the "answer" the company didn't waste a lot of money to develop a worthless property.

Once these two projects were done – the datacentre consolidation and the geostatistical ore body analysis – the IT strategy was completed.

That would have been the opportune time to decide "what's next," but it didn't really happen. Base metal prices (nickel, copper, zinc) began to drop and stayed low for a number of years after that. Most of Sherritt's income came from these commodities, so the new IT strategy had to be to "pull in our horns." There was no cash flow or opportunity to develop anything new. We hunkered down and found ways to continually reduce the spending on IT assets that were already in place.

A Steering Committee of five stakeholders (including me) was in a position to decide what alignment ought to look like. All of us agreed the new IT Strategic Alignment amounted to efficiently operating what we already had, and dreaming about what new things we could do when base metal prices were high enough to provide enough cash for investment.

Chapter 6 Strategic Alignment

Strategic Alignment summary

In order for IT to "do the right things," these must be seen to be so by the leaders of the enterprise – the colleagues of the CIO. So the CIO has to communicate these in a suitable form of IT roadmap and get consensus that the map does indeed reflect the right things for IT to do. That's Strategic Alignment.

The best form that I have seen of an IT roadmap is a strategic and operating plan. This is a multi-year budget wherein the first year is relatively detailed – much like any other annual budget – and all other years of the multi-year planning horizon are less detailed.

For each year of the strategic and operating plan, the IT department outlines the projects it will deliver, the existing systems whose performance it will improve (by means other than an IT project; all the improvements of existing systems requiring an IT project will appear in the project portfolio), and the new capacities and capabilities that the IT function will develop so as to be ready for future initiatives in the enterprise strategy.

The strategic and operating plan will also include a budget by internal department and expense class, staffing plans, and assumptions about future events and circumstances. These will be quite detailed for the first year, and of a more summary nature for the remaining years of the plan.

At the end of the day, the important factor is the understanding and agreement of the CEO and the rest of the enterprise executives that the IT roadmap as presented, is the one that they will support with funding and staffing.

That's all there is to it.

Getting to it is the challenge, especially if the enterprise is not very disciplined or very sophisticated about its own strategic plan. Under those less than ideal circumstances, it is mandatory that the CIO work effectively at drawing out "the right things to do" from his/her boss and his/her colleagues. Otherwise, no matter how good a job IT does delivering new solutions, they don't substantially support the strategy of the enterprise, and so will be misdirected money and effort.

CHAPTER 7 ADVANCED TOPICS

IT organizational considerations

This is not intended to be a comprehensive treatment of how the IT function could or should be organized within an enterprise.

For one thing, there appear to be many works published on this topic, and a lot of advice is available. One more voice added to this learned and thoughtful chorus would be of minimal utility. So I don't cover federated IT organizations, other forms of customer-centric structures, the merits of a purely functional structure or any of the other useful and interesting topics regarding IT organization that are already well articulated by others.

For another, with apologies to the folks that provide this thoughtful and learned advice, I believe that organizational structure is not really one of the key issues that will drive success or failure for the IT function. It is a useful tool to be applied when all or most of the really key issues are already worked out.

In this section I set out a few of the organizational issues, and what I believe from my personal experience to be useful approaches to them. The rest, as they say, is left up to your own judgment and situational analysis.

Is IT a strategic function?

At a CIO conference in Phoenix, Arizona, sometime in the early 1990s, I sat in on a symposium on IT Strategy by F. Warren McFarlan, a long-time professor at Harvard Business School. I don't remember much of what he had to say, but one simple and useful idea stuck.

He provided a quick assessment as to whether IT actually is a strategic function to your organization, and whether therefore it actually requires an executive level manager – a CIO – to run it. A version of the two-by-two chart that he used to illustrate the point appears below.

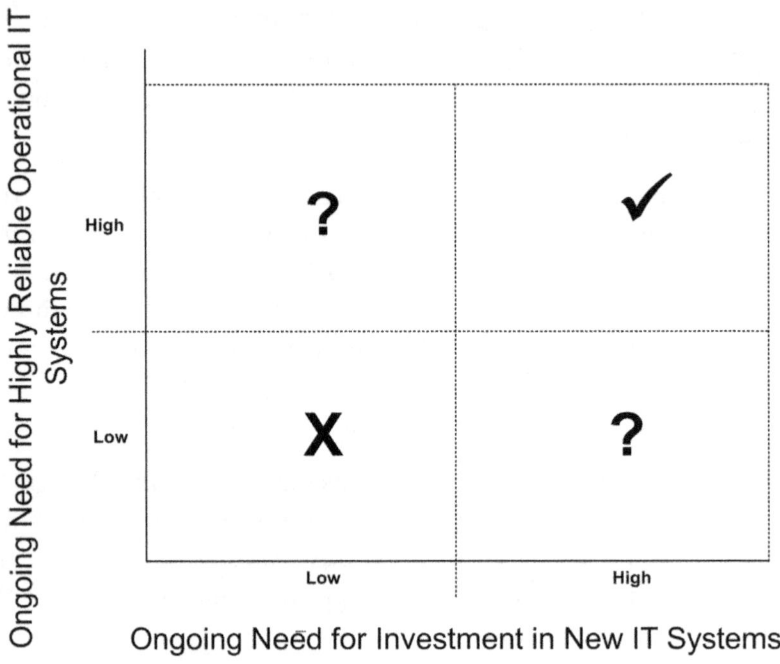

Figure 7 - Determining strategic nature of IT

The professor reduced IT to two basic functions – Solution Delivery (projects delivering new or improved IT assets) and Service Delivery (getting the best value out of IT assets already in place). How important they are to the enterprise at any given point in time – how critical they are to the future success of the entire enterprise – defines whether IT is strategic, and therefore requires a C-level executive.

The chart puts the enterprise's dependence on the highly reliable operation of existing IT systems on the Y-axis and its need for ongoing investment in new IT systems on the X-axis.

If the enterprise's current well-being and future success is dependent upon a "high" need for either one of these, but not both, then the IT functions' strategic nature is questionable (hence the ?).

If the need for both is "low" then IT is definitely not strategic (hence the X).

If the need for both is "high" then IT is "definitely strategic" to the enterprise. If so, then the enterprise definitely needs a "C" level executive to manage the function in order to successfully deliver its IT needs.

So whether IT is determined to be strategic also helps to answer the next section's question. But first, an illustrative example.

A Bombardier Aerospace example

When I took on the role as head of IT at de Havilland, it was my fourth CIO job. I had reported in each previous case to the CFO of those enterprises which were, in order, a mining company (Sherritt Gordon Mines), a wire and cable manufacturer (Canada Wire and Cable) and an auto parts manufacturer (Magna International).

When I was first hired, I worked for one of my predecessors, Kingsley. He was VP of Program Management – a role designed to manage program management for the various Dash-8 vehicle programs and IT. Bombardier took over de Havilland a few months later, changed the organization, and Kingsley left. As a happy consequence, I reported to the CEO of de Havilland for the better part of two years.

Then came the fateful day when I was told that I would be reporting soon to the CFO – a 25-year Bombardier veteran who had been transferred in to de Havilland from the Challenger jet program some months before. I had rather enjoyed reporting to the Chief Executive of a substantial enterprise. My work had been appreciated at that level, and my self-esteem didn't suffer either. Naturally, I fought the organizational change.

My resistance was indulged by the great powers for a little while. Then I was invited to the office of André, the CFO of de Havilland, for a fireside chat.

First, he asked me if my concern was with him personally. I assured him that wasn't the case and I was completely sincere. André was an affable, straightforward and direct person. In the few months that I had worked with him, I had found that he was quite reasonable, a good listener, and could be persuaded to change his mind if the facts supported such a turnabout. Like all of us, he had his prejudices. In his case they were strongly in favour of maintaining positive cash flow, but no one can begrudge a CFO that kind of predisposition.

That being the case, he pointed out that everywhere else in Bombardier – aerospace, recreational products (Skidoo/Seadoo) and in the rail car business – IT reported to the CFO. He didn't think that we could convince anyone to make de Havilland an exception. So why, he said, didn't he and I just go with the flow and avoid a lot of pain and suffering with almost zero likelihood of success?

For his part, he enjoyed finance and knew or wanted to know very little about IT. Since we were stuck with each other, he suggested we make the most of it. If I agreed to keep IT issues and complaints "out of his face," he would help me with politics and networking within Bombardier. Since he had 25 years with the company and knew all the movers and shakers very well, this was quite a generous offer.

And so it was that I went quietly after that conversation. We each kept our side of the bargain, and I would say that it turned out to be a very successful collaboration for André and Al. But for the last few years of my tenure as CIO of de Havilland, I reported to the CFO.

At the time, I was persuaded by André's pragmatic and logical argument. Later, this was reinforced by the seminar where I heard F. Warren McFarlan's "Is IT Strategic?" lecture, and by a series of conversations I had with Alain, the newly appointed CIO of Bombardier's Aerospace Group.

As background, you should know that Bombardier built its financials – both budgets and five-year strategic plans – from a number of financial ratios involving direct costs and two levels of overhead. IT and facilities were functions that made up the costs of the second level of overhead – the overhead on the overhead so to speak.

In summary, Alain's argument was that if IT was successful, it would progressively and inevitably work itself out of a job. Most IT investments at Bombardier were intended to reduce overhead one way or another. IT's budgets were ratio'ed off the primary overhead, so the IT budget base was shrinking and would continue to do so. QED. His intention was to get out of IT and to get into operations as soon as possible.

These conversations were largely meant to be humorous and bantering, but they had the sting of truth to them. In any case, both this banter and F. Warren McFarlan convinced me that at Bombardier Aerospace, IT was not a strategic function. An important one without any doubt, but not a critical success factor for the enterprise's success.

Who should the CIO report to?

If the CIO reports to the CEO then, rightly or wrongly, the enterprise signals that IT is a strategic function. If it does not, then also rightly or wrongly, the enterprise indicates that it does not believe that IT is a strategic function. The purpose of the preceding section is to set out a way by which one can tell which of these possibilities should apply.

Where IT reports is an important factor in what skills and biases the whole function takes on, and therefore how IT performs in the long run. So it is a very important issue for the enterprise to establish clearly and objectively where IT reports – that is, who is the CIO's boss? Does IT report to the CEO? Does IT report to one of the Chief Executive's direct reports – such as the CFO, which is one of the more traditional situations? Or does IT report more than one level down from the CEO?

The success of IT depends a great deal on the personality, management talents and leadership style of the CIO and those of the executive team s/he happens to be part of, probably more than on anything else. However, there are some practical considerations of the reporting relationship that should be taken into account. A "seat at the table," if warranted, is one of these. The reporting relationship should be thought of as a factor that may make it easier or more difficult for a talented CIO to work effectively within a capable executive team. This is self-evidently important in the case when IT is a strategic function.

What if it's not? As much as it pains me to say so, there are many more situations where IT simply is not strategic to the enterprise than where it is. That's not to say it's unimportant – just not strategically so. So what then?

The question then is what bias does the enterprise want to introduce into the role of IT?

Where any service function reports, and IT is certainly no exception, predisposes that service function to accept and internalize the parent function's assumptions about what's important and what's not. In reporting to the CEO, IT as a whole begins to adopt the attitude that it should focus on doing and delivering things that will directly advance the enterprise's long-term goals; anything else is a distraction. It seems clear that's a desirable thing in the case where IT is a strategic function. What are the equivalent biases that would apply if IT should report, and actually reports elsewhere?

Having noted that, I suggest that there are three other broad possibilities.

First, as mentioned earlier, the traditional option has been for IT to report to the CFO. The bias of course is cost reduction – eminently so at Bombardier Aerospace as my earlier example illustrates. A typical scenario in this case is that IT systems are necessary for the success of some fundamental functions of the enterprise. These functions are relatively static, warranting little if any innovation or extension. The cost of delivery is a substantial element of overall enterprise expenses. So the desired outcome is to set up an IT function that could be characterized as "doing the same for less." Under these circumstances, IT reporting to the CFO, an executive with a strong bias in favour of positive cash flow, is a rational organizational structure.

Second, while not really strategic to the whole enterprise, IT might be thought of as strategic to a significant part of it – to product fulfilment, or service fulfilment for Operations or Customer Service just as examples. So some form of operational excellence would be the desired bias. Everyone may agree – explicitly or implicitly – that IT is not strategic and so should not take up any of the CEO's precious management bandwidth. If by default IT then reports to the CFO, problems are likely to arise. The financial bias over IT to "do the same for less" may be appropriate and helpful if the dominant element of operational excellence is product or service cost. If some other elements are just as important, then IT needs to be biased to something more like "do more for the same." Under these circumstances, IT reporting to the COO, or whichever executive is the head of its "biggest customer," would be the more rational organizational structure.

Third, IT may neither be strategic to the whole enterprise, nor may its value to the enterprise fit either one of the two scenarios above or some equivalent approximation. In such circumstances, who cares where IT reports?

The internal organization of IT

The preceding will let us work out, for most situations, where IT and therefore the CIO ought to report. What should the organization reporting to the CIO look like?

"Form ever follows function." What's true for the architecture of buildings, is also largely true for other constructs including IT organizations. That allows for a lot of variation given the many purposes to which an IT organization may be asked to perform. However, there are three guidelines that I have found helpful over time to structure IT.

Major functions

The first is to generally follow the IT governance model that I outlined earlier. That is, in general terms there should be three major functional areas of IT – Architecture, Solution Delivery (IT projects) and Service Delivery (IT operations). It is logical to also consider Strategic Alignment as a fourth major function since it's one of the four major process groups I identified earlier in the simple governance model of IT. Personally, I think that alignment is best performed as a set of functions that are integral to the three major teams, but it's easy to imagine that there could be circumstances where Strategic Alignment as an independent fourth major function would be a rational choice.

Time spans of tasks

The second is to apply the concepts of time span analysis. That is, organize teams under senior managers who report to the CIO according to the targeted duration of a "typical" task to be performed by a member of the team.

By this rule, the Head of IT Operations (Service Delivery) would manage one or more teams who concern themselves with tasks of relatively short duration, such as resolving incidents, managing change requests and engaging in root cause analyses – tasks that typically take a few hours or days. A team member can reasonably be expected to successfully handle many of them in a given day. The Head of Service Delivery would therefore be concerned with the performance of these teams and how it would be reflected in the next few months' worth of performance reports.

By contrast, the Head of IT projects (Solution Delivery) would manage teams who concern themselves with tasks of substantially longer duration. A team member would be expected to deliver a completed result, moving the overall project forward to completion, on average every week. It's rare for a successful project to require provision of deliverables more frequently than every week over its duration. In any case, major phases of a single project might take several months to complete. The full project over all phases will take a year or more to complete. The Head of Solution Delivery would therefore tend to be concerned with a given budget year's projects and how well they are progressing.

Finally the Head of Architecture would manage a team that looks out into the future for several years. A member of the team may be required to project when certain technologies or techniques might be appropriately introduced into the enterprise and under what circumstances. By and large the Architecture team's activities, from the perspective of their time span, substantially resemble those of Projects. Many of them indeed are typically in direct support of work that the Solution Delivery team is delivering. Many others, such as tracking the viability of a technology of interest, would not culminate for several years – when the technology actually does deliver the results desired at the cost point required, or clearly never will.

So when deciding which teams should report to which major IT functional heads, keep task time spans in mind. To be internally synergistic and successful, all of the teams within these functional areas should be consistent in this respect.

Sizing teams for continuity

The third is to consider team sizes for maintaining continuity. This is not a particularly complex idea, but it is amazing how little attention is paid to it and what a high price IT organizations sometimes pay for failing to do so.

As a rule of thumb, when establishing a team that has a common set of accountabilities, make the team no smaller than four. Preferably set the minimum at five. It can of course be larger if the capacity required warrants it, up to the limits of the manager's span of control.

Why a minimum of four or five? Well, what if one team member leaves, or is sick for an extended period, or even goes on vacation? The rest of the team will be expected to pick up the slack. If the team consists of three people, then the two remaining team members will have their workload increased by 50%. Or some work will simply be postponed. This situation will last until the third team member returns or is replaced and the replacement is brought up to speed. Do you imagine your team members or their customers are going to be happy during this period? Yet by keeping the team that small, you pretty much guarantee that this situation of poor service and overstressed staff will happen regularly.

Or do you expect IT professionals to stop regularly changing jobs anytime soon?

What's so magic about a team of four or five? Nothing. The arithmetic of how the remaining members of the team will be picking up the slack is pretty straight forward. With four, each person has to pick up 33% more work. Bad, but more manageable than 50%. Similarly with five, the increment is 25%, which is interestingly just half the incremental work for less than twice the size of team.

The key assumptions are that the team's workload is designed so as to warrant a team of at least four or five and that everyone is cross-trained to do everyone else's job. It's certain that the CIO and his/her management team will have to be pretty creative in terms of workload design for at least some of the teams in IT in order to get to the required minimum size. However, the systematic elimination of service and delivery discontinuity is well worth it.

Change management

As has already been mentioned, successful delivery by IT of the right solution is a necessary but insufficient criterion for the success of the IT investment. It's really as far as the IT organization can go. The rest depends on client management and on the HR organization. They are the ones that have to prepare the part of the enterprise that is affected to take full advantage of the new investment in IT (and in most cases, many other changes to the old way of doing business).

However, in self-defence and in order to influence the prevention of foreseeable failures (see Standish Group's Chaos Report on the root causes of the dismally low success rate of large IT projects), IT needs to raise the awareness of key sponsors about this key issue, to bring forward specific examples of the types of changes that need to be managed by the business sponsors and their staffs, and to smooth the way to successful change as much as possible.

The chart below illustrates the process whereby the parts of the organization affected are prepared for the change.

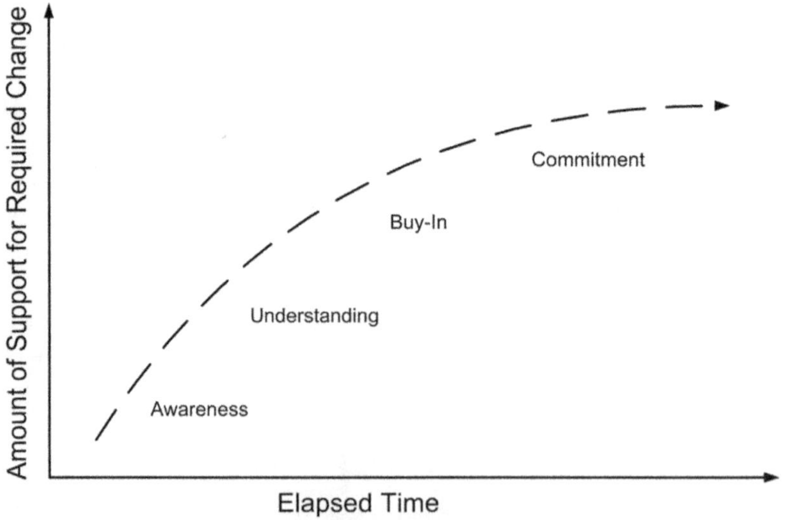

Figure 8 - Model for managing change

The four phases of change are named by the degree of support that they enjoy among those affected. (This four-stage model is by no means the only one available to practitioners of Change Management, but it's the one we'll use in this discussion.)

The first chronologically, "Awareness" can be assisted by the communication plan that appears in most worthwhile IT project plans (See project charter discussions within the chapter on Solution Delivery). The chronological second, "Understanding" can be assisted by the training plan that also appears in most IT project plans.

Note that there is nothing that IT can do to encourage "Buy-in," or "Commitment" with respect to the contemplated change. Creating these attitudes in the staff who are the target of the change is entirely the responsibility of the Executive Sponsor, and those to whom s/he delegates responsibility for effecting successful change in his or her functional area.

Note also that a significant aspect of managing change that is not explicitly called out in the model is some form of confirmation from the change targets that each of the phases has been successful. That is, our IT plans can identify deliverables of the communication plan – who is to create and to deliver them, and when this is to happen. These can all be "ticked off" and calculated as "complete" for tracking purposes, but it's a rare communications plan that also tests whether "Awareness" has been successfully achieved among 100% of the targeted population.

This is even rarer in IT plans (I have never seen it in my experience) for "Understanding." While training is well-covered, and there are often even proficiency tests afterward to confirm that those trained actually know how to use the IT capabilities delivered, this cannot be construed to be complete and successful "Understanding" of all the changes contemplated. It certainly doesn't establish whether this "Understanding" has been achieved in a high percentage of the organization targeted for the change.

Similarly objective and empirical testing for the success of "Buy-in" and "Commitment" are really not usual elements of an IT project plan. But all such testing, and launching of new measures to establish complete Awareness, Understanding, Buy-in and Commitment in the event the initial measures are not completely successful, must be indispensable elements of a change management plan that is necessary to achieve the desired result.

So the CIO and his/her Project Manager should use this, or similar material, to inform the Executive Sponsor of the elements of a successful change management plan, to suggest that one or more suitable experts to create one and carry it out, be retained, and badger the Executive Sponsor to make it so. If change is not explicitly and expertly managed, then it won't happen, any more than anything else that is not managed. This will greatly reduce the probability of success of the investment in IT (among other things) and all anyone will remember was how "IT screwed up."

Yes this approach does sound defensive, and maybe it is. I prefer however, to think of encouraging the enterprise to engage a knowledgeable change manager as "IT Risk Management."

We'll conclude this section with the inevitable story.

Change management at Enbridge Services Inc.

Shortly after the turn of the millennium, I was hired by Enbridge Services – a household appliance sales and service company – on a contract basis, to manage a number of supply chain management projects. Most, but not all of them involved investment in IT. My last project required a substantial re-engineering of business processes and supporting application software in order to rationalize all supply chain management into a single team, versus the multiple disjointed teams that had evolved over the many years that the company had been a captive division of a retail gas distribution monopoly – Consumers' Gas.

The supply chain piece, for which I was responsible was only one part of a much larger integrated program. Much the same changes had to be made to the management of the financials, of the mobile (technicians) work force, of the retail sales, and some other major pieces of the business. So all these projects were put under a Program Manager, and were managed in a co-ordinated way.

The business case for rationalization of processes and systems was compelling. For an investment of $12 million to $13 million, the business could expect to recover around $4 million in annual operating savings. More than half of that would be due to tangible savings in the supply chain side of the operation.

While there was the usual drama and nail-biting that any large and risky project experienced, by and large all went well. The goal of my part of the program was to rationalize and expand all supply chain management capabilities, providing the capability to apply supply chain best practices and thereby provide the means to reap millions in annual savings. We regularly delivered the required scope, hit our timelines and kept our spending under budget. There was only one fly in the ointment.

No leader had been named to run the supply chain organization. Indeed, it had been widely recognized that the experience and talent for such a large role did not exist internally. It had never been needed before, so there was no opportunity for it to develop even as a growth opportunity for a junior person. It had to be recruited externally. Moreover, the new leader would have to structure the organization, manage educating and training for his/her staff, and in short be a change leader as well as an operational leader. There simply was no way to compensate for the absence of that high level of executive knowledge and leadership.

I dutifully flagged it as an issue, and approached the Executive Sponsor – the Chief Operating Officer (let's call him "Larry") – who agreed that the resolution to the issue was to start and successfully complete an external recruitment. Time passed, and the talent search never started. The head office of the enterprise was in one small office building, with a cafeteria on the ground floor and a convenient entrance to and view of the employee parking lot. My office was on the same floor as Larry's. Conditions were ideal to continually remind Larry (an unkind person would say to "harass" him, and that would be accurate). I took full advantage.

It had no effect. The project was coming closer and closer to completion. The "race car" was almost built, but we had no Formula One Mario Andretti available to drive it properly.

Finally I cornered Larry in the cafeteria and went after him without mercy. He got a little red in the face, but remained patient with me. He said something very much like this: "You don't have to convince me. I get it. Every day I leave home with this issue near the top of my list of things to do. Then I get here, and I'm handed a bunch of things way more important than this one. Trust me, they are or they wouldn't get priority. By the end of the day, it just isn't done. Then the process is repeated the next day. Leave it with me. Eventually it will get done."

I really wasn't satisfied. For one thing, I found it hard to understand how the enterprise could have such a wealth of priorities that would trump $2 million to $3 million in annual savings. But Larry had been both clear and firm: back off. So I did.

To make a long story short, sometime later as the project was nearing completion we learned that negotiations had been taking place behind the scenes to sell off the business to a third party. Larry had been one of the key negotiators. The buyer was a much bigger company with a sophisticated supply chain function of its own. So a much bigger change had been taking shape behind the scenes, while I had been trying to rescue the (relatively) much smaller one – a subset if you will.

That made me feel better. I think.

Chapter 7 Advanced topics

Outsourcing

There was a brief discussion of IT outsourcing within the context of "benchmarking." This section goes into the subject in more depth.

The practice of outsourcing major elements of a business to an outside party has a long and largely successful history. It's so commonplace in automotive, aerospace and other manufacturing that it has become part of the DNA of these industries. It has established a strong foothold in services industries such as banking and most other business sectors.

The ongoing drive for competitive advantage is relentless. Any organization in any industry that is not actively considering delegating significant elements of its operations to partners who can bring a competitive edge to the overall enterprise will find itself on the scrap heap in pretty short order.

The IT function was one of the early adopters of outsourcing. This started primarily with farming out computer room operations (the proverbial "raised floor"). It has spread to create a marketplace full of vendors that collectively can capably cover all aspects of IT, up to and including farming out the entire function, CIO included.

Taking all this as a given, then why does outsourcing have such a bad reputation? It's pretty easy for someone who wants to make the point that "outsourcing is bad" by pointing to one or more decidedly dismal horror stories. So what is the truth?

My short and simple answer is that people tend to confuse the "what" with the "how." In that context both can be correct. A good business case (the "what" we should do) is executed poorly (the "how" we should do it). Or even worse, a poor business case is formulated. Then there isn't much that can be done to improve it by any reasonable execution strategy. So both the "what" and the "how" are negative examples.

Lessons from the Trenches

So outsourcing as a whole is deemed to be A Great Thing by the formulators of the business case, and to be A Disaster by those observing the train wreck that (often) is its implementation.

Let me first set out a few points about what outsourcing typically is not.

It is not a means to fix a part of your operation that is out of control, has a bad reputation or is otherwise operating poorly. If it is out of control, it will stay out of control, unless you overtly bring it under control yourself, or engage the outsourcer to not only run it for you but to also bring it under control while doing so. That's definitely two separate, although related, assignments. The scope of work, the terms and conditions and success criteria for both assignments have to be fully understood by both parties, and agreed for both items of work. That especially includes clearly defining what "under control," "now has a good reputation" or "operating well" actually looks like.

Outsourcing is not a means to get rid of one or more "problem children" in your own organization. Unless you actually terminate or reassign the "problem child" beforehand, or make the outsourcer aware of the problem, and make its solution an explicit part of the deal, the problem will continue to be there. You will simply be reducing your ability, afterward, to influence its resolution.

It is not a means to introduce flexibility, agility and nimbleness (FAN) into a part of your organization where it didn't exist before. It will be ipso facto an "arm's length" relationship and so will tend to introduce more formality and a need for more discipline. This doesn't automatically preclude the introduction of FAN as part of the deal, but FAN has to be an explicit part of the deal. And obviously you should never assume that an organization that did have FAN characteristics will remain so after it is outsourced.

Outsourcing ordinarily will not save the organization money. There is no inherent economic benefit to hiring an outside organization to perform work that you are already doing. In general, whatever an outsourcer can do, so can you. That includes running a part of your IT operations for less cost. You may choose to get someone else to drive costs out of a part of your organization because you don't have the managerial capacity, technical knowhow, scale of operations or the cash flow to support investments that may be required to achieve this. IT is no different from other parts of the enterprise where labour is expensive and often capital investment is justified by substituting hardware and software assets for skilled labour. The classic IT outsourcing case is exactly that – outsourcing the "raised floor" operations to someone else who then can reduce the number of people monitoring your consoles, mounting your tapes, etc. They do this by investing in monitoring and alarm systems and other forms of automation that allows them to absorb more work without having to hire as many people as you have doing the same. Again, it's two different scopes of work – one to operate and the other to invest for the purpose of driving out costs in a pre-defined and agreed manner. In the "raised floor" example, the outsourcer gives you a fixed price based on your actual current costs or a little less to sweeten the deal and then proceeds to reduce its costs even further through the means outlined above. The outsourcer's payment is the savings generated. By the end of the deal, there can be a lot of gravy for the outsourcer. Of course, by then they've earned it. But you can do the same if you choose.

Signing on the dotted line of an outsourcing contract is not the end of the story. Every deal has a finite life. There is usually a five-year term to most IT outsourcing contracts, largely because the outsourcer has to make substantial investments at the beginning and requires time to recoup them. Even if the deal is well-formulated with both parties satisfied going in and largely satisfied coming out, five years is a long time. Circumstances change; needs change; and expectations change. Consideration must be given to what will happen after the deal – and not just to one or more extensions to the deal. Assume that at the end of the planned term one or both parties will need a different kind of arrangement. Then plan for it. That's the best possible outcome. Having said that, why would you not plan for something less than an ideal outcome? Especially, not plan for a vendor that does not perform as required? Do not leave yourself "stuck" with a deal that is intolerable to you a year or two into it. The situation isn't any better if the vendor finds itself in a deal that it doesn't like. Arranging for an exit strategy based on various scenarios is a necessary part of an outsourcing contract – like any other arrangement between arm's length parties.

Outsourcing will not eliminate the need to provide management oversight of the deal. Do not ever be so naïve as to assume that an outsourcing agreement will run on autopilot. Someone in your organization has to look out for the interests of your enterprise, and manage the deal according to its metrics and service-level agreements. Do not be so naïve as to assume that the vendor staff will always "do the right thing" by your organization. They are not accountable to you, but to their own internal masters – a different company, remember. Oversight by your own vendor management team will keep them accountable to you – nothing else. Do not underestimate the amount of time and effort required to manage an outsourcing contract. Most of them are quite complex, and no matter how well-crafted or thought out beforehand, unforeseen circumstances inevitably arise. These require immediate management attention, or they will fester. False precedents and assumptions will take root and grow into truly ugly weeds, especially as the outsourcer's management team goes through the normal staff turnover and new faces – without the benefit of being there during the early days of the deal – begin to come on the scene. Start out with much more management oversight than you think you need, and then back off as appropriate. Adopt the opposite approach at your peril.

A non-IT example may be helpful from my time as the CIO of the Magna International seating division in the late 1980s.

Chapter 7 Advanced topics

Automotive outsourcing example

Magna had won the contract to supply seats for the Chrysler minivan to be made in the assembly plant in Windsor, Ontario. At the same time, Chrysler had awarded the seating supply contract for the stretch version of the vehicle which was assembled in St. Louis, Missouri, to a Magna competitor, Lear-Siegler. In effect the two vendors were a backup to each other – a typical practice in automotive outsourcing.

Through various mishaps, Lear failed to provide sufficient product to keep the Chrysler assembly plant continuously operational. As a direct result, barely into the first year of the contract, the "steel snake" in St. Louis was shut down on two occasions, for several hours each time.

Automotive assembly plants in North America in those days typically produced about 200,000 vehicles a year, based on a nominal 1,000 vehicle per day output. About 3,000 Chrysler plant workers were idled for hours. In short, Lear's failure to perform caused Chrysler several millions of dollars of unproductive costs for each incident. The consequences to Lear-Siegler came swiftly and were final.

Shortly after the second incident, both Lear and Magna officials were called to a no-agenda command performance in St. Louis. When we were all there, the Chrysler buyer came into the room and sat down at the head of the table. In very short, declarative sentences he gave us our instructions: Magna had one year to establish a seating plant in the St. Louis area, within that time to deliver parts that passed the Chrysler quality specifications, and to continue to supply Chrysler's requirements to the end of the contract term. Lear-Siegler's management would continue to supply seating until Magna was ready to take over. Lear would co-operate fully with Magna's project plans or suffer further financial consequences. End of discussion.

Lessons from the Trenches

What does this case have to do with IT? Not much, but then as I mentioned at the beginning of this section, outsourcing is not limited to IT, nor are the general principles of what constitutes a well-structured deal limited to an industry or to a business function. It is meant to be an instructive general management comparison. Outsourcing of a part of your operations – whatever they are – has to follow much the same business imperative, whether it's aerospace, automotive or IT.

Was this an example of badly executed outsourcing? Lear-Siegler certainly faced serious consequences for poor performance. It had to write off a lot of plant and equipment that suddenly had little value, and to forgo millions in lost revenues after Magna took over. But Lear was the outsourcer and Chrysler was the client. Lear's failure to perform certainly did cost Chrysler a considerable amount of money and embarrassment in the marketplace. On the other hand, Chrysler had recourse under its contracts to execute an exit strategy. So for Chrysler this was just a bump in the road in what overall was a very successfully outsourced operation. Luckily for Chrysler, its backup, Magna International, performed satisfactorily for both the Windsor and the St. Louis operations.

So what lessons should be drawn from this?

That's simple: do have the conditions for a breach of contract clearly defined; do have the transition process fully defined beforehand in case of a breach or any other reason, including normal completion of the planned term, also clearly defined and agreed beforehand, in as much detail as you can think of – and your high priced consultants can think of; and don't "hope for the best" by not doing this work.

Yet how many IT outsourcing contracts are written without consequences to the outsourcer for a failure to perform? Or without a viable and detailed exit strategy for the customer if the failure to perform is protracted or particularly egregious?

Hands up, all those who have had experience with a poorly performing outsourcer? Now, hands up all those who have had experience with an outsourcing contract where there were no significant consequences for poor performance? Just as I thought; it's pretty much the same set of hands.

There are many good books written, complete with illustrative case studies, about outsourcing – "how to" and "how not to." I therefore won't dwell on this topic any further, except to draw an additional analogy to which I alluded earlier. Entering into an outsourcing contract is very much the same as hiring a new manager for a part of your IT function. The job has to be well-described. The work has to be clearly delegated. There has to be a regular review of performance, based on clear and mutually agreed metrics. And if performance is consistently below defined expectations, then a performance improvement program must be put in place. Ultimately, if the new manager is unsuccessful at turning him/herself around during the course of the performance improvement program, termination is in order. Why would you not take at least the same care on the same issues with a third-party?

Professional certification of IT staff

You as a CIO are an executive of a substantial enterprise. You are dependent upon a team that is disciplined and motivated. One of the most powerful tools available for the motivation of staff is to have the enterprise tangibly and visibly support their professional development. And one of the best sources of discipline for your professional staff is to have them adopt one or more of the available professional disciplines through certification.

Actions always speak many decibels louder than words. By providing financial support and by supplementing that by enthusiastically investing your own time and theirs into actively encouraging, supporting and celebrating their professional growth, you will demonstrate your wholehearted commitment to excellence.

The certifications I have spoken of earlier in this book – PMP from PMI, various ITIL certification levels, TOGAF and Zachman, CBAP from IIBA (there are many others, more concerned with technical skills and abilities, which I haven't cited since this is a book on IT management) – all cost an individual several hundreds and sometimes thousands of dollars to buy study materials and to pay for and attend lengthy testing sessions. Not to mention the hundreds of hours of personal time an individual has to invest in order to master the material sufficiently to pass the qualifying examinations. Most of these certifications also require a commitment to an ongoing effort to maintain the individual professional's standing, once successfully certified.

All of this is quite a daunting burden for an individual professional.

I have found that both financing and otherwise supporting professional certification within an IT department pays huge dividends in motivation and staff morale, well beyond the individuals who may be pursuing a certification at any given point in time.

Financing is usually not much of an issue, since most organizations these days have an educational policy that covers these costs. However you, as the CIO will probably have to make sure that you have the funding within your own departmental budgets to take advantage of the policy.

Supporting these individuals by giving them the time to attend special (and expensive) prep courses, as well as the tests themselves more tangibly demonstrates your commitment to their professional growth. A still more tangible demonstration of IT management's commitment is the encouragement of "lunch and learns," and other forums where both aspiring certificants and the already certified professionals share knowledge and experience with the new knowledge and practices.

Such forums can easily be organized around "what's new in the profession." Since most of these certifications evolve – especially some of the newer ones such as the CBAP for Business Analysts – there is no lack of raw material. They can also be organized around the need to standardize internal methodologies or outcomes, or simply to bootstrap the capabilities of themselves and their colleagues. Professionals can review examples of their own recent work, and decide what should be "best practices" internally.

And you, as the CIO should participate in those discussions and support them by changing internal process per their recommendations. It would be better that neither you nor any member of the IT leadership team take an active role in actually organizing and running these activities. They should be self-managed by fellow professionals. Limit your participation to encouragement behind the scenes, funding, and active participation in the events and activities that they organize themselves. In this case it is more effective to be an enthusiastic follower. It's a rare organization that doesn't have at least one or two individual-contributor professionals more than willing to lead this sort of thing and I frankly have never come across any place without such voluntary leadership. I believe that this is empirical validation of my basic premise that given half the chance, IT professionals far prefer to exert themselves to pursue excellence than to practise Mordacism of any kind.

Finally, in summary regarding support to the professional certification of your professional staff – just do it. No more pusillanimous arguments.

Chapter 7 Advanced topics

Completed staff work

If you are unfamiliar with the concept of "completed staff work," I highly recommend that you acquaint yourself with it as soon as you can. It is an elegantly simple idea, which is incredibly well-suited to management in general, and to information technology management specifically.

While it is easily explained, I am recommending that you don't depend on what's written in this book about it. I'll give you the basic concept, but the idea will root itself more firmly in your mind if you do the small amount of research and reading yourself. It will be well worth your while.

Simply google the section heading. You should find a Wikipedia article online as well as find the original U.S. and Canadian Army memorandums that set out the idea during the Second World War.

There are also articles illustrating how Henry Kissinger and others applied the concept to their own particular subordinates during their own careers. Stephen Covey writes in his usual clear and compelling style about this subject. I strongly suggest that you research all these and get a good solid idea of what it's about, and then apply it. Insist that your whole IT management team applies it.

Briefly, here it is. Completed staff work is the work done by a subordinate to put in front of his/her superior to get a decision of any kind. The clearest example is to decide on a solution to a problem. So the subordinate must clearly state the problem, and set out all the viable options to resolving it and their pros and cons. And the subordinate recommends one of the options, with the rationale for the recommendation. His/her superior should not require anything beyond this analysis to make a sound decision. It is not expected that the superior will always accept the recommendation. S/he is expected to have a different perspective than the subordinate and will therefore weigh the analysis differently than the subordinate who prepared it. But the fact that the superior chooses a different option than the one recommended by the subordinate in no way represents a failure on the subordinate's part. Failure or success is purely determined by the completeness of the analysis.

Completed staff work encourages people to do their own thinking and to put only their best work forward. It produces clearer and higher-quality work by tapping into your team's talents and potential. It specifically provides you, the boss, with a useful strategy to resist the placing of the monkey on your back by your staff. Keep the monkey firmly on their back. Coach them to think and communicate their own way through a problem and the several practical options that exist to resolve it before they make a recommendation to you.

The reason I point this concept out as being particularly applicable to IT is because people within it, more than most other groups, tend to hide behind technical terms and jargon. Fancy and faddish terminology is too often substituted for real thought or real communication. All management and professional staff should be taught the doctrine of completed staff work, and the reasons why it is especially applicable to the practice of information technology. Any IT staffer at any level who can't express him or herself in terms of "completed staff work" should be "kept out of the face" of decision makers other than their immediate boss – especially those outside of IT.

Ignore this advice, and you face the consequences of constantly cleaning up the messes your subordinates will create for you.

Chapter 7 Advanced topics

CIO, CTO, CKO – What's in a title?

The focus of this book is to discuss and to teach the fine points of the role of the Chief Information Officer from the point of view of somehow who has managed to survive in the trenches for a lengthy period. The CIO is the most senior manager in the enterprise responsible for information delivery, as briefly explained in "The Role of IT," above.

There are a couple of other titles bandied about that have quite a different meaning, and describe quite a different kind of role. There is no consensus as to the meaning of these titles, or the roles they are intended to describe. They are even newer than CIO, so what I will be presenting as definitions are certainly arguable. Perhaps one day I will be able to claim credit for properly defining these new roles "back in the day" before a consensus formed around their meaning.

The Chief Technology Officer (CTO) is the Chief Engineer of an IT software or services company. Just as a Chief Engineer designs products for sale by a manufacturing or an engineering company, the CTO does the same kind of thing for an IT company.

Alternatively, in some larger companies the Head of IT Architecture is sometimes given the CTO title. I think there is some logic to this, but fundamentally, I consider this to be confusing. It confuses the role of IT architecture with IT product or service development.

The Chief Knowledge Officer (CKO) is an even more recent role and title. It presupposes an organization is not only "promoting" data to information, but is further "promoting" information to knowledge. The CKO's role is therefore to facilitate that second "promotion" and to make this augmented repository of knowledge easily accessible to whoever in the organization needs it.

As a practical matter, both the definitions of information and of knowledge are in the eye of the beholder, so the CKO would need to work very hard at consensus building within the organization. Also as a practical matter, very few businesses have been able to beneficially define "knowledge" and a way to apply it for the benefit of their bottom line.

In my experience, only law firms fall into this category. Some of the larger multi-office and multinational law firms have a CKO. The "killer app" for these firms is a system to organize and retrieve complex documents such as contracts relevant to particular clients and situations. The payoff is minimizing the net new work to be done by a lawyer to prepare such a contract once the initial one has been created and entered into the "knowledge base."

In theory accounting firms, engineering firms and other professional services organizations would benefit from a similar "knowledge base" in much the same way as a law firm. However, few law firms actually have an executive titled "CKO," even though many of the larger ones have some version of the application described above. Most of their information technology chiefs are titled "CIO," and indeed "killer knowledge app" or not, the role fulfilled is really the CIO's as described in the rest of this book.

So, avoid the confusing, faddish and often inappropriate use of "CTO" and "CKO." Stick to the solid, clear and completely understandable sobriquet of "CIO."

Chapter 7 Advanced topics

A capability and maturity model for IT

As mentioned in an earlier section, when I set out to write this book I had no intention to address the topic of a capability and maturity model. Indeed, the concept of a CMM for IT goes so far beyond my impression of its state of the art, that the idea never even occurred to me until I received a thoughtful comment to one of the blogs serializing parts of this book, more or less suggesting that it would be a good idea, and why.

It is probably a very good idea, but not one that I feel qualified to formulate and articulate on my own. A better approach, it seems to me, would be for a group of like-minded peers, current and former CIOs all, to consider the subject as a group and to see if a consensus can be formed around what the capability and maturity of an IT function would be defined by. Then these qualities of an IT department could be structured to provide a scale whereby IT departments could be ranked.

We have two major challenges to overcome before we can confidently start formulating such a model for broader application. The first and probably more tractable challenge is to find a way to objectively measure the capability and performance of Architecture (I'm thinking something along the lines of the trend over time of some form of total cost of ownership). The second, and to my mind the much more difficult one, is to find a way to objectively measure the effectiveness of Strategic Alignment.

So I'm challenging readers of this book, qualified as indicated above and interested in contributing to this idea, to contact me as volunteers for this work, or to "voluntell" others to join me in a group to do so.

Once this group forms we can agree on how to communicate and publicize our thoughts on the subject. One way might be to write a sequel to this book, sharing the further experiences of several of us.

CHAPTER 8 SUMMARY AND CONCLUSION

At last we are at the end of this little book about the art and science of senior IT management. You should now have quite a comprehensive view of what is required to be a successful CIO.

You should now understand that "what you don't measure, you don't manage." Opinion and conjecture about how well IT is delivering solutions and service to the enterprise are frankly for amateurs. Professional IT managers employ quantitative measures, and lead IT according to these facts.

You should also now accept that whether or not IT is doing good quality work, is entirely based on the client's perspective. In order to help make this a practical perspective, IT performance measurement must be transparent and visible to the client. The measurement should be developed and presented in a manner understandable to the client and relevant to the client's business.

You should now more fully appreciate the importance of comprehensively good management within IT, and what that entails. As the overall leader of IT, you should be delegating your responsibilities to an excellent team of managers who are all well suited to carry out the roles you give them. You should support and develop them where they are weak, and help them shine where they are strong. Finally, you should be sufficiently committed to the success of the organization to swiftly and humanely remove those individuals who are clearly unable or unwilling to carry out their role or to work in collaboration with the rest of your team.

You should now be able to organize your management team to "do things right" according to the simple and practical model of IT governance that was expounded upon at length in these pages (or your own adaptation of it). You should be able to explain to your Architecture, Solution Delivery and Service Delivery teams what their roles are, and how they must collaborate with each other to deliver successful IT investments that support the strategy of the enterprise, now and in the foreseeable future.

Finally, you should be able to draw out of your colleagues in the enterprise, through a methodical Strategic Alignment process, what are the "right things to do" – those IT projects and initiatives that the business truly needs in order to successfully achieve its strategic goals.

It must be recognized that IT management is an unusually challenging and demanding human activity. In my view, it is much more so than most if not all, other areas of management within the typical enterprise. The case for this is somewhat "between the lines" in the preceding pages of this book. Before closing I will very briefly try to make it more explicit for you.

In comparing IT to other back office functions, such as human resources and finance, the management of IT is much more challenging in that neither of these two functions has in its mandate the requirement to either build or operate any artifacts critical or otherwise relative to the ongoing health of the enterprise. Only facilities management (or facilities engineering as it is sometimes named) is required to fill a similar role, and this is only rarely. Many manufacturing enterprises, and most utilities (taking enterprises such as the Greater Toronto Airports Authority) require a facilities function to perform something similar to the IT role in that respect. Outside of these two sectors, such a role for Facilities is rare, whereas for IT it is common in almost all types of enterprise.

In my view, this makes management of IT more demanding than almost anything else. Give this idea some thought, and if at the end of it you disagree, please drop me a line. I would appreciate hearing any counter-argument.

To return to a theme that was set out in the Introduction, information technology is a relatively new field of human endeavour. It has grown rapidly over a few decades into an enormous field of activity that requires many different technical specializations and professions to deliver all that it can offer. Indeed, it continues to grow in size and complexity as Moore's Law continues to apply – by now it seems to be like one of Newton's laws of physics. As the relative cost of IT continues to fall, human ingenuity and initiative applies it in new ways for economic and social benefit.

Ever smaller enterprises can profitably implement large and complex software applications, such as enterprise requirements planning for their back office administration and customer relationship management for their front office administration that once only very large and wealthy enterprises could take advantage of.

Sophisticated software applications such as computer aided design (CAD), computer aided manufacturing (CAM), computer aided engineering (CAE) and robotics have become much more sophisticated and much less expensive, making it feasible for ever smaller-scale manufacturing and industrial enterprises to compete on a global scale, without much regard for the cost of labour.

Banking, once dependent completely on a local presence in myriads of branches, thanks to relatively inexpensive but very sophisticated information and communications technology now can be conducted globally with absolutely no need for "bricks and mortar" facilities to interact with customers.

The advent, growing sophistication and global reach of the Internet has made it possible for very small, geographically dispersed enterprises to band together synergistically and effectively with collaboration and communication tools into larger virtual organizations that can compete effectively in most if not all lines of business with large global enterprises.

Chapter 8 Summary and conclusion

With commonly available eCommerce software tools, small enterprises with a single geographic location, can effectively and economically conduct business on a global basis, where once that would have been completely infeasible.

One can easily add to the list of capabilities that are rendered "faster, better, cheaper" by the application of information technology. Please feel free to do so. There is no lack of examples. There is great promise in currently, and soon-to-be-available new information technologies to do just that, and new examples seem to be created almost daily.

Yet this promise is too often thwarted. Why? Why is there this perceived gap between the great potential benefits of investment in IT and the often disappointing reality?

If you have read this far and still can't answer this question, then you haven't been paying attention. Or you're being sarcastic, so quit it.

I believe that it is due to inadequate management in the IT function. This opinion is based firmly on the experiences and observations of a working lifetime that spans almost all the time that information technology developed from something very rare and esoteric to its pervasiveness today. The one constant that I have observed during that period is the relatively poor management of the IT function. This is true in absolute terms and certainly is true relative to the unusual demands that the IT function places on its management teams.

I have gone on at length, and I hope helpfully, on a number of the more typical weaknesses. At the beginning of this chapter, I summarized what I believe are the remedies for these weaknesses and what amounts to a recipe for success for the new CIO.

My hope is that you have enjoyed reading this book as much as I enjoyed writing it. I look forward to feedback from readers, especially from other CIOs, whose experiences I would love to hear about. In particular, I would enjoy collaborating with other seasoned CIOs on an effort to establish an easy to understand capability and maturity model for IT management.

God bless, and Godspeed.

GLOSSARY OF ABBREVIATIONS

Abbreviation	Full term
Admin	Administration
BABOK	Business Analysis Body of Knowledge
CAB	Change Advisory Board
CAD	Computer Aided Design
CAE	Computer Aided Engineering
CAM	Computer Aided Manufacturing
CBAP	Certified Business Analysis Professional
CEO	Chief Executive Officer
CFO	Chief Financial Officer
CIO	Chief Information Officer
COBIT	Control Objectives for Information and Related Technology
COO	Chief Operating Officer
COTS	Commercial off the shelf software
CRM	Customer Relationship Management
CWC	Canada Wire and Cable
ERP	Enterprise Requirements Planning
FAN	Flexibility Agility Nimbleness
GM	General Manager
HR	Human Resources
IIBA	International Institute of Business Analysts
ISO	International Organization for Standardization
IT	Information Technology
ITIL	Information Technology Infrastructure Library
PC	Personal Computer
PM	Project Manager
PMBOK	Project Management Body of Knowledge
PMI	Project Management Institute
PMP	Project Management Professional
QCS	Quality Cost Schedule
QED	Quod erat demonstrandum

Abbreviation	Full term
RASCI	Responsible Accountable Support Consult Inform
RFI	Request for Information
RFP	Request for Proposal
SAN	Storage Area Network
SDLC	Systems Development Life Cycle
SLA	Service Level Agreement
SMART	Specific Measurable Agreed-upon Relevant Time-bound (referring to Goals)
SME	Subject matter expert
SOW	Statement of Work (sometimes Scope of Work)
SSO	Shared Services Organization
SWOT	Strengths Weaknesses Opportunities Threats
TCO	Total Cost of Ownership
TOGAF	The Open Group Architecture Framework
UAT	User Acceptance Test
VP	Vice President
WAN	Wide Area Network
WBS	Work Breakdown Structure

www.ingramcontent.com/pod-product-compliance
Lightning Source LLC
Chambersburg PA
CBHW031927190326
41519CB00007B/435

* 9 7 8 0 9 9 4 8 4 4 2 0 0 *